= 1 = 75'

4/11

MORE GOLF SECRETS

MORE
GOLF SECRETS

Sequel to
THE GOLF SECRET

by
DR. H. A. MURRAY

PAPERFRONTS
ELLIOT RIGHT WAY BOOKS
KINGSWOOD SURREY U.K.

SALE CONDITIONS

This book shall only be sold, lent or hired for profit, trade or otherwise in its original binding, except where special permission has been granted by the publishers.

Notice to Readers

Every effort is made to ensure that "Paperfronts" are accurate and that the information given in them is correct. However, information can become out of date, and authors' or printers' errors can creep in. This book is sold, therefore, on the condition that neither Author nor Publisher can be held legally responsible for the consequences of any error or omission there may be.

Made and printed in Great Britain by
Cox & Wyman Ltd., London, Reading and Fakenham
and published by
Elliot Right Way Books, Kingswood, Surrey

CONTENTS

DIAGRAMS

PREFACE

As a golf professional of more years experience than I care to remember, I have no hesitation in saying that Dr. Murray's second golf book does indeed warrant the title "More Golf Secrets".

The author has given the reader the benefit of his long experience of the game by approaching the subject in this book in the same analytical manner as he did the swing and golf fallacies in "The Golf Secret".

The grip and the stance I have never seen so perfectly and completely described.

Ball spin and its effects are fascinating and instructive.

Putting, the stymie, and the chip-shot—the all-important "short game"—are admirably described with a view to "rolling three shots into two".

Shots from the rough, uneven lies, and bunker shots are made to appear almost desirable for the pleasure they give, and the mathematics of them are intriguing and convincing. Wind and rain no longer seem to matter.

The skilful analyses of the various golf factors provide much information that is entirely new.

This book is a "must" for every golfer—rabbit or tiger.

ALGY EASTERBROOK.

INTRODUCTION

SINCE my book "The Golf Secret" dealt with only the swing and numerous golf fallacies, I determined to "fill in the gaps" by writing a sequel to it in the same critical strain. "More Golf Secrets" provides all the remaining answers.

Professional teaching regarding the grip, the stance, and many other things described in this book is almost as contradictory as are expert ideas of the swing; while bunker play, shots from the rough, and awkward lies are usually treated in a perfunctory manner. I have dealt fully with these and other subjects, so that the reader will have no difficulty in mastering them, and consequently will find that golf really can be easy; but he should first read "The Golf Secret", and thus acquire a reliable grooved swing, as a "solid foundation" on which to build.

The two books together constitute a reliable treatise without the usual contradictions, controversies, doubts, and consequent difficulties; and therefore fill a long felt want both for high and low handicap players.

No doubt, as with the swing, you will prefer to profit by my past mistakes rather than your own, by reading "More Golf Secrets".

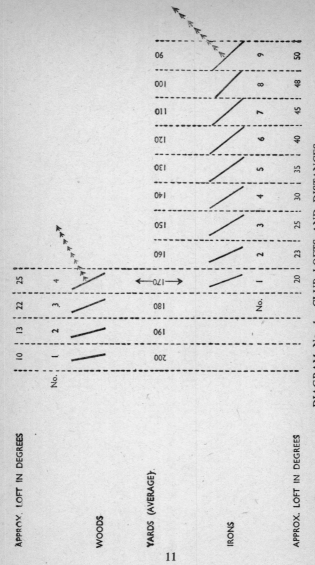

DIAGRAM No. 1.—CLUB LOFTS AND DISTANCES

ARROWS REPRESENT FLIGHT OF BALL, AT RIGHT ANGLES TO CLUB FACE

11

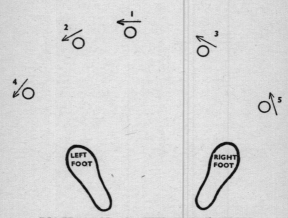

DIAGRAM No. 2.—THE FIVE STANCES

THE ARROW BESIDE EACH BALL INDICATES ITS DIRECTION OF FLIGHT

With Ball position No. 1, feet in square stance; Nos. 2 and 4, closed stance; Nos. 3 and 5, open stance. A straight shot is possible with any stance providing the left shoulder points to the target (square "shoulder stance"), and the swing is correct. A square foot stance is the more dependable because then a square "shoulder stance" is more natural. Remember that it is the shoulder position that governs the direction of the ball's flight.

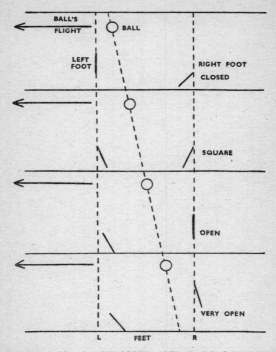

DIAGRAM No. 3.—STANCES AND BALL POSITIONS

An interesting discovery emerges from studying this Diagram. In such a series of stances, from closed, through square, to open, the golf balls, if in their correct positions, form a straight diagonal line. Diagonal because the ball should be nearer left foot with a closed stance and nearer right foot with an open stance, than the intermediate square stance position. If the closed stance shown in the diagram were less closed than depicted, the ball would still be on the "diagonal line", and therefore a little more to the right.

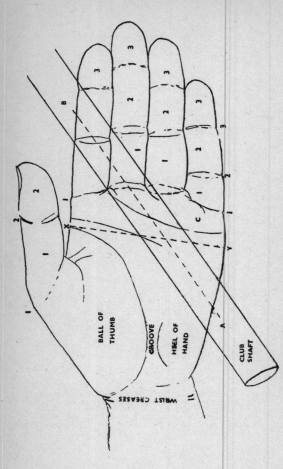

DIAGRAM No. 4.—ELEMENTARY ANATOMY OF THE HAND

1, 2, AND 3 =FIRST, SECOND, AND THIRD CREASES AND SEGMENTS OF FINGERS
A–B =CENTRE OF CLUB SHAFT
X–Y =LINE OF KNUCKLES
C =CALLUS

First step in taking the grip is to apply the left hand at an angle of 45 degrees to the front of the club shaft, as in the diagram. For subsequent steps, see text.

14

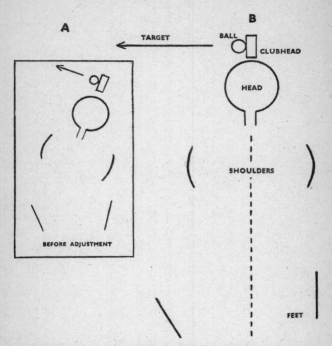

DIAGRAM No. 5.—STANCE FOR PUTT, CHIP-SHOT, AND
STYMIE. OVERHEAD VIEW

"A" depicts the danger of pushing the ball to the right by playing these short shots
with a square stance. With the excessive, though desirable, back bending, the high left
shoulder is nearer the target line than the right one.

"B" shows the open stance described in the text, which renders the "shoulder stance"
square, and puts the club head midway between the heels—these two factors ensuring
accuracy.

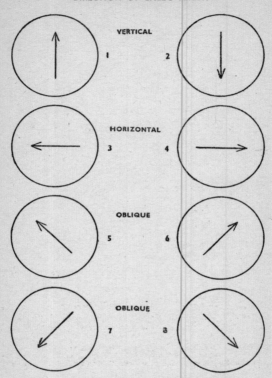

DIAGRAM No. 6.—BALL SPIN

The arrows on the "golf balls" indicate the direction of spin. 1. True top spin. 2. True back spin. 3. Horizontal clockwise spin. 4. Horizontal anti-clockwise spin. 5. Oblique clockwise top spin. 6. Oblique anti-clockwise top spin. 7. Oblique clockwise back spin. 8. Oblique anti-clockwise back spin.
Causes and effects described in the text.

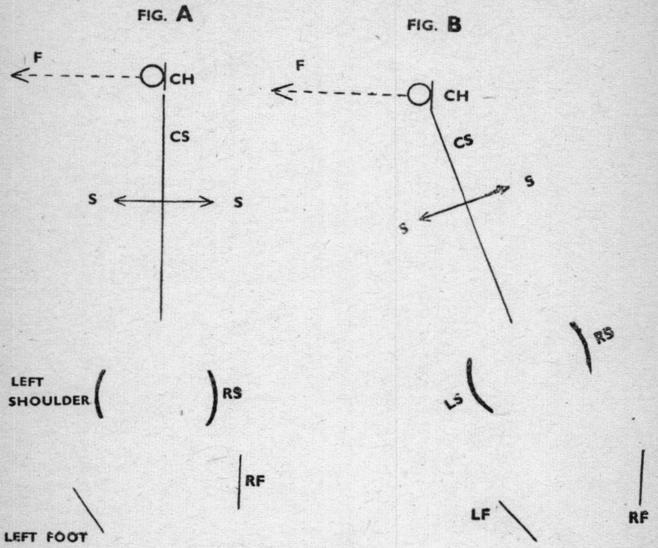

DIAGRAM No. 7.—THE CUT-SHOT

LF = Left Foot.   RF = Right Foot.   LS = Left Shoulder.   RS = Right Shoulder.   CS = Club Shaft.   CH = Club Head.   SS = Direction of Swing.   F = Flight of Ball

Position of feet and flight of ball are the same in both figures.

Fig. A: Ordinary shot played with square club face and open stance, but shows the wrong ball position for the cut-shot caused by faulty conception of playing the cut-shot with open stance.

Fig. B: Correct conception of cut-shot, played with square stance aimed to the left, the ball being farther to the left. "Cut" and direction of flight are governed by the open club face facing target, in conjunction with the "square stance swing" aiming left. The correct ball position and consequent left shoulder position are the secrets of success.

17

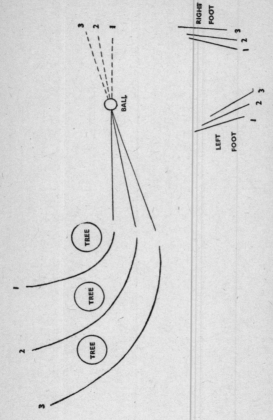

DIAGRAM No. 8.—THE INTENTIONAL SLICE

Shows three square stances aiming progressively to the left of the target, the ball travelling progressively farther, before turning to the right. In all three instances, the club face is "open", and a normal "square stance swing" executed.

18

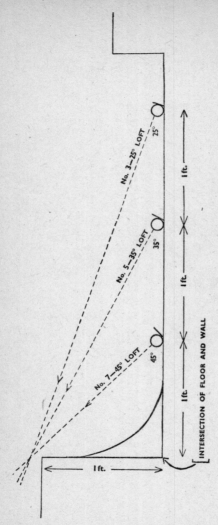

DIAGRAM No. 9.—BUNKER SHOTS

Depicts a bunker with front wall one foot high and golf balls lying on the floor, one, two, and three feet from the intersection of floor and wall. Also shown is the appropriate club to use to just clear the wall, together with the club's loft and the ball's elevation. Notice that the angle formed by the flight of the ball and the ground, is always the same as the loft of the club used.

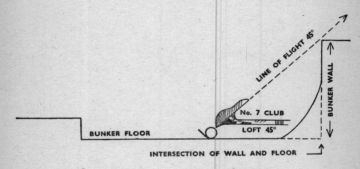

LINE OF FLIGHT 45°

BUNKER WALL

No. 7 CLUB
LOFT 45°

BUNKER FLOOR

INTERSECTION OF WALL AND FLOOR

DIAGRAM No. 10.—BUNKER SHOTS

Shows a method of gaining experience in determining which club to use to make the ball just clear the bunker wall. Description in text.

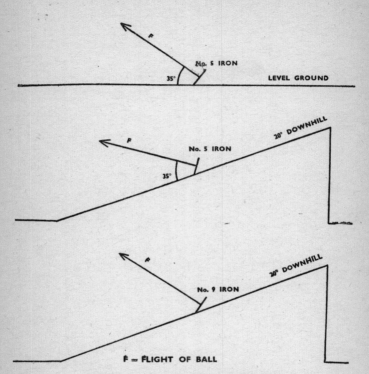

DIAGRAM No. 11.—DOWNHILL LIES

A given club will always produce the same angle between the ground where the ball lies and the ball's flight, therefore on a downhill lie a more lofted club must be used to counteract the loss of ball elevation.

21

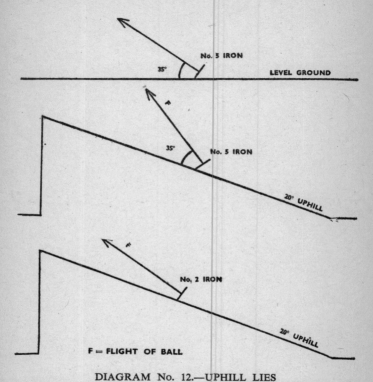

No. 5 IRON

35°

LEVEL GROUND

F

35°

No. 5 IRON

20° UPHILL

F

No. 2 IRON

20° UPHILL

F = FLIGHT OF BALL

DIAGRAM No. 12.—UPHILL LIES

The requirements here are opposite to those for a downhill lie, i.e., a less lofted club must be used to counteract the increased ball elevation and consequent loss of length.

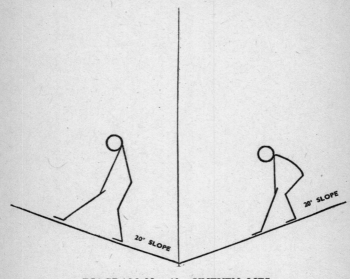

DIAGRAM No. 13.—UNEVEN LIES

FEET BELOW BALL

Legs forward at ankle, making smaller angle between leg and foot.
 Weight more on toes.
 Knees forward, relatively above toes.
 Seat above heels—standing position.
 Back practically straight.
 Shoulders high.
 Hands more forward.
 Arm–club shaft angle larger.
 Club head and ball farther from feet.

FEET ABOVE BALL

Legs back at ankle, making larger angle between leg and foot.
 Weight more on heels.
 Knees back, relatively above heels.
 Seat behind heels—sitting position.
 Back very bent.
 Shoulders low.
 Hands less forward—lower down.
 Arm–club shaft angle smaller.
 Club head and ball nearer to feet

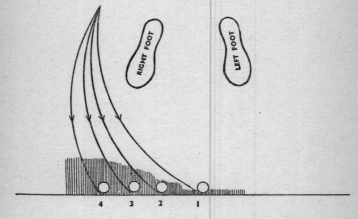

DIAGRAM No. 14.—SHOTS FROM THE ROUGH

1 = FAIRWAY
2 = SLIGHT ROUGH—OFF FAIRWAY
3 = MEDIUM ROUGH—LONG GRASS, ETC.
4 = HEAVY ROUGH—GORSE, HEATHER BRACKEN, ETC.

Note the ball position in relation to the feet, progressively to the right as the rough becomes worse, also the progressively earlier impact with ball before the bottom of the swing arc.

CHAPTER I

THE STANCE, BALL POSITION, AND ADDRESS

THE stance, and its concomitant parts, are not usually dealt with in sufficient detail.

Under ten separate headings I will endeavour to make the subject perfectly clear, and to explain "how" and "why".

THE SET

Perhaps ninety per cent of golf's difficulties are due to the fact that the left hand is higher than the right one on the club shaft, making—in effect—the left arm about three inches longer than the right one.

If it were possible to grip the club with our right and left hands at the same level, we would then stand absolutely square, with both shoulders level, and strike the ball just in front of the centre of the stance.

But, as things are—and must be—the hand position necessitates "the set", which in turn necessitates contacting the ball somewhere to the left of the centre of the stance. Therefore to ensure the club shaft being at right angles to the intended direction of flight at the address, the hands must be moved to the left.

This causes the right knee to bend a little more, and a little more weight to be on the left foot; and—most important—movement of the left shoulder either upwards, backwards, or both. Since on the forward swing the left shoulder must go up, that has an important bearing on the manner of assuming the set.

If you grip a club, and take up a square stance with your shoulders level—i.e., both the same height—your hands will be opposite the right half of your body, and the club will be pointing about forty-five degrees to the right. The club can be brought into the correct address position by drawing the left shoulder (i.e., the left corner of the body) either upwards or backwards. It should be done by moving the left shoulder in the direction in which you intend to hit the ball—that is, upwards.

Do that, and you will see your hands move straight to the left, and in fact all other parts will automatically fall into place; including a backward movement of the left hip and a forward movement of the right hip, in exactly the same manner in which the hips move as you pull up the left shoulder during the forward swing. This produces the effect of a square stance with the feet, a square or slightly open "stance" of the shoulders, and an open "stance" of the hips. Remember that these automatic adjustments are only slight, and that many players tend to exaggerate them by consciously imitating some detail in a photograph.

If you made the mistake of taking your left shoulder backwards instead of upwards, you would see your hands move in a slight curve to the left, which is a forerunner of an outside-to-in forward swing, and a consequent slice.

The correct assumption of the set as described causes the body to curve somewhat, with a convexity to the left.

That, then, is the set, and how it is done, and why. It does not consist of a complicated series of separate movements. It is done simply and naturally merely by raising slightly the "left corner of the body" until the club head is behind a correctly positioned ball.

THE SHOULDER "STANCE"

In whatever position you place your feet—whether square, open or closed—always have your shoulders practically square to the target. That is to say, the line through your shoulders should be parallel to the intended direction of the shot. In other words, point your left shoulder to the target.

You must do that if you intend to play a normal straight-forward shot by pulling the left shoulder up on the forward swing.

If you played a shot from an open stance, with your shoulders as well as your feet turned to the left, you would be aiming to the left of the target. In that event the only way you could play straight for the target would be to make the left arm and hand lead the whole way in the follow through without any wrist-roll at all—i.e., a "push shot".

You can prove that it is the shoulder line that ultimately determines the direction of a normal shot by studying Diagram No. 2. This shows that a shot *can* be played in the same direction whether the "foot stance" be square, open, or closed, providing the left shoulder is pointing at the target.

By keeping the feet in the position indicated, and turning the body left to address ball No. 2 (Diagram No. 2), you will be in the usual closed stance. By turning the body back to the right until you address ball No. 3, you will be in the usual open stance. By addressing ball No. 1 you will, of course, be in the square stance. By turning the body to the left to address ball No. 4, you will be in an extreme closed stance; and by turning to the right to address ball No. 5, you will be in an extreme open stance.

The point is, that with all these stances—and every possible intermediate one—it is possible to play a straight shot to the same target, providing you start with the left shoulder pointing to the target, and swing merely by revolving your shoulders around the upper part of the spine.

The extreme positions 4 and 5 are, of course, impracticable, but the obvious restriction of the forward swing in

No. 4, and of the back-swing in No. 5, serve to demonstrate at least one disadvantage of any open or closed stance.

There is another point to be considered regarding the position of the shoulders. When addressing the ball, both shoulders should be brought forward towards the chest, into the flat-chested, round-backed position. This will bring the elbows, as well as the shoulders, nearer together into the approximate position which they should occupy at impact.

Neglecting to do this will make you stand too near to the ball, with the risk of "shanking" it if the shoulders come forward—which is very probable—during the swing.

For obvious reasons, if you are blessed (or cursed as far as golf is concerned) with wide, square, set-back shoulders, you start at a distinct disadvantage as compared with your narrow-shouldered, flat-chested friend.

RELATIONSHIP OF ONE FOOT TO THE OTHER

Whatever stance you adopt, whether square, open, or closed, your feet should always form the same angle to one another as they do when you walk. They should be parallel if you walk that way; they should form a large angle—maybe ninety degrees or more—if you are "splay-footed"; they should be turned in if you are "pigeon-toed"; and they should make a moderate angle—maybe forty-five degrees—if you are average.

It is no use copying other people in this respect. You must adopt your own "foot-angle". The importance of this is that our feet are turned "in" or "out" by movement chiefly in our hip joints and to a slight degree in our knees when they are bent.

The movement of turning the feet "in" or "out" is limited. For instance, you cannot "point your toes" backwards. Therefore the right hip "locks" when the movement is complete towards the end of the back-swing; and similarly the left hip locks towards the end of the forward swing.

Obviously, to turn either foot "in" at the address would restrict the swing in that direction; conversely, to turn either foot "out" *beyond its normal walking position* would delay the hip-locking which normally "tightens the spring" on the back-swing, and provides the resistance to the blow on the forward swing.

How this hip action, through the position of the feet, influences the position of the body can be well demonstrated as follows: Stand upright in a square stance with both feet turned out naturally—just as you walk. Keeping the heels on the ground, turn the left toe "in" until the left foot is parallel with the right one. You will then find that even though your stance is still square by the "toe-line", your chest in its natural position is facing half-right in a similar direction to your toes. Then turn both toes to the left, and your body will be facing half left.

That demonstration serves to show that if you put your right foot at right angles to the intended line of flight (as frequently advised), and the left foot, say, forty-five degrees to the left—even if the stance is square—then the chest and shoulders will be turned at least "quarter-left". Stated otherwise, you are playing an open stance, though you think it is square.

This further demonstrates the disadvantage of any stance other than square, because even if you adopt a square "shoulder stance", say with an open foot stance, the shoulders will at least tend to turn left about impact, owing to the hip joints trying to get into their natural positions.

It is clear, then, that for all straightforward shots both feet should be "turned out" if you walk that way.

There is another aspect of the relationship of one foot to

the other; namely, the distance they are apart—i.e., the width of the stance.

I am not alone in believing that a wide stance is best. Among others, Ben Hogan recommended it. A wide stance will probably make you feel more tightly "wound-up" at the top of the back-swing—which is all to the good.

A good guide as to a suitable width of stance is the feeling experienced in the right leg at the top of the back-swing. If the right leg is then nearly vertical and you feel that you could stand on it alone, then the stance is too narrow. There is a much more powerful feeling when the right leg slopes outwards from the hip to the foot, so that you are certain that you could not stand on that one leg. From that position the weight moves much more freely to the left on the forward swing, with a feeling of a tremendous amount of body—and power—in the shot.

This feeling can be likened to "kicking off" with your feet against the wall of a swimming-bath, except that in the golf shot the "footwork" is automatic. The position of the right foot merely gives you a "good grip of the earth", thus serving as a safe and secure fulcrum for the start of the forward swing. There must be no conscious pushing with the right foot.

A wide stance is supposed to restrict the "pivot"; and it is sometimes supposed to be desirable to restrict the pivot for a short shot. Therefore, according to these two suppositions, we should use a wide stance for a short shot and a narrow stance for a long one! Very confusing, and very contradictory. But actually, I believe the suppositions apply only to a flat swing, in which a wide stance does undoubtedly restrict what is usually called the "pivot".

With the better upright swing, which most professionals use via a horizontal upper part of the spine, I find that the important "shoulder pivot" is not restricted by any reasonably wide stance.

A wide stance is preferable, thus providing a broad base, and thereby assisting balance by making it easy to keep the hub of the swing in the same position and augmenting the feeling of swinging upwards on the back-swing and upwards on the forward swing.

In some golf books we are told to narrow the stance progressively as the clubs become more lofted, but I have never been able to discover any sound reason for this, which seems to me needlessly to complicate the game.

For example, many if not most professionals at the top of the back-swing for a full shot with any club have the shaft about horizontal, therefore, since any full shot requires the same amount of effort, I believe the same wide stance should be used with all clubs.

Maybe it is justifiable to narrow the stance for "part shots" if you feel more comfortable that way, since there is then less force in the swing, and therefore less body movement due to momentum, and so less need for a broad base. But I don't consider it necessary to make it a rule. I see no advantage in having the heels nearly touching for a chip shot—rather the reverse, since a more accurate shot is likely with a more secure base.

The main criterion is to feel comfortable, and to have the feet wide enough apart to have sufficient "grip of the earth" for the job in hand.

A working rule might be: a wide stance for maximum effort with any club, and as wide as comfortable for less effort.

RELATIONSHIP OF THE FEET TO THE TARGET LINE

This is what is usually referred to as "the stance", of which there are three varieties—closed, open, and square. See Diagrams Nos. 2 and 3.

Closed Stance. From the square stance the right foot

is drawn back one or more inches. A line across the toes will then point to the right of the target.

The only thing that prevents the ball from being pushed out to the right is the fact that it is positioned farther to the left than with a square stance, thus producing a square "shoulder stance".

This stance is calculated to produce a hook to the left, because the club head tends to traverse an exaggerated inside-to-out course. The ball is therefore struck a glancing blow, which causes an anti-clockwise spin to the left, which in turn causes the ball to curve to the left.

A straight shot can be hit with this stance, but it is more difficult for most people. It is supposed to produce a long shot with a low trajectory, and to assist a player who has difficulty in completing the pivot. That is true enough if you think of pivoting the *hips* with a flat swing, but it is unnecessary if you concentrate on a shoulder pivot around a horizontal upper part of the spine, and thus swing upright.

Why use a stance which is calculated to produce a hook, when you wish to play a straight shot?

Open Stance. This is the opposite to a closed stance, both in appearance and effect.

From the square stance the left foot is drawn backwards one or more inches. A line across the toes will then point to the left of the target.

The only thing that prevents the ball being hit straight to the left is the fact that it is positioned farther to the right than with a square stance, thus producing a square "shoulder stance".

This stance is calculated to produce a slice to the right, because the club head tends to traverse an outside-to-in course. The ball is therefore struck a glancing blow, which causes a clockwise spin to the right, which in turn causes the ball to curve to the right.

A straight shot can be hit with this stance, but it is more difficult for most people. It is supposed to produce a shot of high trajectory, and to assist the player who has difficulty in getting his left side "out of the way". This is true enough if you think of pivoting the *hips* with a flat swing, but is unnecessary if you concentrate on a shoulder pivot around a horizontal upper part of the spine, and thus swing upright.

Why use a stance which is calculated to produce a slice, when you wish to play a straight shot?

This stance is more dangerous than a closed one, because it is probably true to say that everybody, when they start to play golf, swings outside-to-in, and therefore has a ready-made slice.

Very few novices hook accidentally, or even can do so intentionally, but they can all slice. In addition, the slice is known to be the commonest fault in golf, and often creeps back into the game of even scratch players.

I know that the open stance gives a feeling of confidence because you are partly facing the target which you wish to hit. But this is a snare and a delusion against which I have had to fight. Often, for a time, I have thought, "open stance for me", until half of the shots sliced to the right, while the other half pulled to the left.

Some professionals—even if they use a square stance for long shots—advocate progressively opening the stance as the clubs become more lofted, claiming that this makes the swing more upright. Another illusion! With an open stance the earlier pull on the left hip during the backswing restricts the automatic hip turn, and therefore also the automatic shoulder *turn*, consequently the club goes less far back and the swing *appears* to be more upright; and may result in an outside-to-in forward swing. (Actually, with any stance the back-swing *automatically* becomes progressively more upright as the club shaft becomes

B

shorter, in consequence of the inevitable progressively increased back-bending.)

The shortened back-swing due to restricted automatic hip turn resulting from an open stance has led to the erroneous belief that the back-swing should be deliberately shortened as the club loft increases. But action photographs of many experts reveal that for a full shot with any club the club shaft is in approximately the same position—i.e., horizontal—at the top of the back-swing; therefore it would appear that some of them do not practise what they preach.

Any slight advantages of the open stance are far outweighed by the disadvantages, such as a marked tendency to slice, the possibility of hitting the ball to the left as though from a square stance aimed to the left, and the acknowledged difficulty of correctly positioning the ball.

In my opinion the open stance should be used only for the cut shot, and for the "putting group" of shots: the putt, the chip, and the stymie—i.e., the very short shots.

As an object lesson we will compare golf with the less debatable game of tennis.

You will always see the "rabbit" partly facing the net (open stance) for a forehand drive. Consequently he knocks the ball across court—or out of court—or with insufficient strength to get it over the net because there was no body-power in the shot. On the other hand, the "tiger" plays with a square stance, pointing his left shoulder in the intended direction of the shot, and consequently putting his body into it.

Square Stance. With this, which might be called the mathematically accurate stance, a line across the toes is parallel to the target line.

I have already shown—by implication—why the square stance is the best and most natural, and the least liable to error and complications.

Since it is to-day used almost universally by professionals and other top-class players for long shots, we can accept that as final.

Doubt arises only when we consider the shots "through the green"—broadly speaking, iron shots; for which we have already discussed the uncertainties and pitfalls of other stances.

Apart from the fact of being more reliable, the square stance for all shots adds greatly to the simplification of the game, which I believe has been made needlessly complicated, and to appear, in consequence, to be more difficult than it is.

Golf becomes relatively easy and a pleasure with one stance, one swing, almost one ball position which is easily found, an easily found target line with consequent accuracy, and only one thing on which to concentrate—i.e., the left shoulder.

It must not be forgotten that some professionals—among the world's best—do advocate and use the square stance for all shots. Also I believe that many others do not open the stance nearly so much as readers of their books imagine. I am sure I am not the only one to have noticed—often with annoyance—that photographs in golf books are almost invariably taken at such an angle that it is impossible to know the exact stance used.

There is one other very important aspect of the relationship of the feet to the target line. It is no easy matter to assume the stance you intend. Many people think they are "standing square" when in fact they are in an open stance. The test is to put a club across the toes to mark the target line.

I have often done it myself after taking up what I thought to be a square stance, and on "looking along the club" have been surprised to find that I was aiming to the left. The mistake is nearly always to the left, because it is natural to turn the body a little to the left when, from the stance, you look to your left for the target line. Conversely, "left-handed" players would tend to aim to the right.

But there is no need for this difficulty, for the target line is easily found if you take the trouble to look for it in the obvious way.

I will describe how I do it with every shot from the drive to the putt. As I walk towards the ball from behind, I get the ball exactly between myself and my target. Then, while still walking, I look for a particular spot a foot or so behind the ball; it may be a few blades of darker or paler grass or a piece of soil—there is always something that you can fix with your eye. Keeping an eye on that spot, I put my feet down—in the stance—with toes parallel to the line from the "spot" to the ball. In the case of a putt, the spot is picked in front of the ball, and used to "roll the ball over", with due allowances.

Having probably convinced the reader that he should use a square stance, I will admit that there are exceptions to this, as to all good rules. Readers of "The Golf Secret" will know that correctly initiating the forward swing by pulling the left shoulder upwards, produces *automatically* the desirable inside-to-out swing. Now with a small minority of players their natural inside-to-out forward swing, thus produced, will be *too much* inside-to-out; so that at impact the club face will be facing slightly to the right, consequently the ball will finish to the right of the intended target.

If you are one of those people, do not try to correct this tendency by altering your grip if you know it to be correct, as that would cause confusion and inconsistency. The proper correction is to open the stance—but only slightly—which will render the swing less inside-to-out, thereby bringing the club face square to the target at impact.

This turning of your whole body to the left must not be overdone, or you will then swing outside-to-in with a consequent slice. If your ball is finishing, say, ten yards to the right of your target, that amount of error would probably be corrected by drawing the left foot back only one inch from the square stance; but each player in this category must ascertain by experiment the degree of open stance necessary to correct the error.

Don't think of this as playing with an open stance, but rather as a slight turning of your whole body to the left at address, to counteract the effect of your natural though extreme inside-to-out swing, thereby causing the club face to be at right angles to the target line at impact, as—of course—it should be.

RELATIONSHIP OF THE FEET TO THE BALL POSITION

Those who play tennis or table tennis will know the difficulty of returning a ball that has nearly passed the body. It is generally scraped over or chopped, without freedom of body movement and without power. Even with the right-handed tennis forehand drive it is best to contact the ball a little to the left of the middle of the body. Obviously this is even more necessary with the predominantly left-sided game of golf, in which—for a straightforward shot—it should be always somewhere between the centre of the stance and the left heel.

Approximately midway between these two points could reasonably be called "the standard ball position" for a full clean iron shot without a divot, while one inch or so to the right of this would be a suitable position for an iron shot with a divot. An inch or so to the left of the "standard position" would be the usual place to contact the ball with a driver, because the face of the driver is slightly ahead of the shaft, and because it is usually considered desirable to contact the ball with a driver a little past the bottom of the arc.

With the driver, some professionals tee the ball an inch or two to the left of the club face at address. To all whose drives are mediocre—in fact to all who have not tried it—I would recommend trying this method, with a ball tee-d as high as the peg will allow, and one, two, or even three inches in front of the club head, which is grounded—note well—normally at the bottom of the arc. The idea is to give the ball a flat blow without spin, just as the club head is rising; instead of back spin, which would produce a higher shot, or top spin, which would cause the ball to come quickly to earth.

A common mistake is to vary the ball position too much with different clubs, although it is necessary—and admittedly difficult—with stances that become progressively more open or closed.

See Diagrams Nos. 2 and 3, in which it will be seen that with a closed stance the ball should be farther and farther to the left as the stance is more and more closed; while with an open stance the ball should be farther and farther to the right as the stance becomes more and more open.

With a closed stance, if the ball is not enough to the left, it will probably be pushed out to the right when struck, or it might be "spun" to the left.

With an open stance, if the ball is not enough to the right, it will probably be "pulled", or hit straight to the left, or it might be sliced. Remember that with the left foot drawn back, say, two inches, the "toe line" extended for a shot of perhaps a hundred yards will finish a long way to the left of the target. That open stance with the ball not enough to the right is the reason why so many approach shots to the green finish in a bunker on its left flank. That is no doubt why the golf-course architect placed the bunker there.

A great advantage of the square stance is that the ball position is easily found and need not vary at all with different clubs, beyond the aforementioned two positions— for driver, and clean iron shot, or iron shot with a divot.

A square stance begets accuracy and keeps you out of bunkers!

There is another aspect of the relationship of the feet to the ball position—that is, the distance you should stand from the ball. The frequent advice that the end of the shaft should touch the left knee is nonsense, particularly so since most people use clubs that are too long for them.

The thing to remember is not to "reach" for the ball, and this is particularly important with the upright swing.

With correct body-bending, the arms should be hanging perpendicularly, or nearly so, thus preserving the angle between the arms and the club shaft. If the centre of the club face is not then behind the ball, don't adjust it with your hands or arms, but do it by slightly moving your feet either nearer to or farther from the ball.

It should be remembered that *the correct ball position for any shot is just in front of a "correctly positioned club head"*.

Don't be a slave to measured positions for the ball (such as "two inches inside the left heel"). The positions which I have described should be regarded as a guide, to demonstrate how little, if at all, the ball position need vary.

When you are satisfied that your body is in the correct position and the correct "set", with the club shaft at right angles to the intended line of flight, if the ball is then not immediately in front of the club head, move your feet until it is so, then you will contact the ball at the true bottom of the arc.

RELATIONSHIP OF THE GRIP TO THE STANCE

The best stance in the world will not produce a good shot if the grip is wrong.

Assuming the stance to be correct, what are the possibilities other than a straight shot with a grip other than correct?

1. If the whole grip is too far to the right, the club face will shut at impact, resulting in a hook or smother.

2. If the whole grip is too far to the left, the club face will be open at impact, resulting in a slice and a shot of high trajectory.

Other mishits depend on wrong positions of one hand, and which side of the body is in control.

3. Left side in control, left hand too far to the left—a slice.

4. Left side in control, left hand too far to the right—a hook or smother.

5. Left side in control, right hand too far to the left—probably a normal shot, maybe a slice.

6. Left side in control, right hand too far to the right—probably a normal shot, maybe a hook.

7. Right side in control, left hand too far to the left—the shot might be reasonably good, especially with a flat swing, because of more wrist-roll, but anything could happen.

8. Right side in control, left hand too far to the right—probably a hook or a smother.

9. Right side in control, right hand too far to the left—a slice.

10. Right side in control, right hand too far to the right—a hook or a smother.

If you multiply the above possibilities by the number of possible stances, you will begin to realise why there is so much bad golf played.

There are still more possible results due to "letting go" at the top, which is caused by not gripping tightly enough at the beginning.

It would surely appear to be wise to become thoroughly accustomed to one stance—unvarying—and to stick to it for all shots.

Also, I have said enough to persuade the reader that a correct, unvarying grip is essential, but that will be considered later.

USE OF THE FEET

With the correct upright swing there is little or no toe-to-heel weight transference, and any that does occur is not impressed upon your consciousness; therefore there is no likelihood of falling forwards or backwards. For that reason you will probably not need to think of your feet at all, except to stand normally.

It will nevertheless be useful—for certain shots to be described later—to understand the two methods of obtaining a firmer grip of the earth, one of which is essential if you swing flat, since there is then a tendency for the impetus of the forward swing to throw you on to your toes towards the ball.

One method is to put definitely more weight on to your heels than your toes. This will counteract any tendency to fall forwards, and will also prevent too much left heel raising on the back-swing. Sometimes I wonder why we have heels on any shoes. We would be more naturally on our heels maintaining the correct angle between foot and leg if we wore heel-less shoes such as bowlers wear. Playing golf in bowling shoes is well worth a trial by anyone who habitually "falls forward".

The second method is to grip the ground with your toes, and I would emphasise that the two methods cannot be used together, because you cannot grip with your toes if you have more weight on your heels.

Algy Easterbrook, the eldest of the three golf professional brothers, told me many years ago that the inner

soles of many professionals' shoes had well-marked toe
impressions, due to gripping the ground. I will describe
how the reader can demonstrate for himself how this is
done, and how it works.

To grip anything with your fingers, you must bend them
towards the palm of your hand. Demonstrate this by
putting your hand palm downwards on a table, then press
your finger-tips on to the table and draw them towards
your palm. While doing this ask someone to lift your hand
from the table by putting one finger under your hand.
You will find that he cannot do it. Then stop gripping, and
he will lift your hand quite easily.

Now, the toes can be made to grip the ground in exactly
the same way. I think this must be the *modus operandi* of
the young lady on the Variety Stage who apparently
makes herself light or heavy at will. Test it in the following
manner.

Get two friends to stand one on either side of you, while
you stand naturally with your arms perpendicularly down
by your sides, but with your forearms bent up at the
elbows. Ask them each to put a hand under your elbow
and lift you off the floor. They will do it with ease. Then
ask them to do it again, but before they do so draw back
your toes—as you did your fingers—in an effort to "grip
the floor". Your friends will be surprised to find that you
have become much heavier, and, in fact, they may be quite
unable to lift you.

That, then, is the way to grip the ground with your feet,
thereby giving yourself a secure base—if required to that
extent—on which to swing the upper part of your body.

Apart from the foregoing preparation—which may even
not be necessary—the feet are not consciously used at all.

Not only should the left heel remain low down on the
back-swing, but there should be no active heel-raising or
foot-pushing during the entire swing. Any such happen-

ings are all automatic and do not require any conscious assistance from the player.

THE KNEES IN THE ADDRESS

For all shots, both legs should be bent forward at the knees. This is important, because in the bent knee a certain amount of twisting movement is possible, which becomes less so as the leg is straightened, until finally the knee is completely locked backwards.

Most of my readers will have either danced, fenced, skated, boxed, or played table-tennis or tennis, and will know that the knees are always bent during these activities.

This knee-bending is universally acknowledged to be equally important in playing golf, but what appears to have been overlooked, even by the experts, is that the amount will vary with different people; and also the connection between this knee-bending at address and the right-knee position at the top of the back-swing and on the way down. Proof of their oversight is the fact that some professionals make much of a straight right leg at the top, while others are equally insistent that it should be bent.

From studying photographs of experts, I find that apparently those who bend their knees most at the address have more right knee bend at the top and also more knee-bending—i.e., they "sit down" more—during the early part of the forward swing. Once this is pointed out, if anyone takes the trouble to think, it is what you would expect! Ossie Pickworth may not have thought of this as a possible explanation for the bent left knee which he advocated *after* impact.

Examine experts' photographs in various stages of the swing, and you will find "plus knee-benders" at address to have the right knee bent at the top of the back-swing and who "sit down" more on the forward swing; also "minus knee-benders" with a straight right leg at the top and with less sitting down on the forward swing.

What lesson do we learn from all this? Simply that it is no good copying one professional's very bent knees at address, and another's very straight right leg at the top of the back-swing; and no use trying to "sit down" on the forward swing if you have little knee-bending at address or at the top.

Actually, all you have to do is *to find the amount of knee-bending at address which suits you*, then remember that the other positions will occur automatically. I will only add that there must be some knee-bending at the address, and better too much than not enough.

THE ADDRESS

Most professionals advise applying the club head to the ball as it is approached from behind, and then adjusting the stance or foot position. With that I am in entire agreement, if you can do it, and also remember to bend your back and not straighten your wrists.

I have often seen players address the ball in this professional manner, and then lift the club to waggle, unbending their backs in the process, and finally grounding the club with their hands—instead of again bending their backs—thus to some extent "undoing" (i.e., increasing) the angle between their arms and the club shaft. They wonder why they top or mishit the ball!

A much safer method is to take a good firm grip while standing behind the ball, then, maintaining the semi-crouching attitude and also the angle between the arms and the club shaft—the upper arms being lightly against the body—walk towards the ball. Having taken up the approximate stance in this position, the club head will probably be a little higher than the ball. Don't alter the shaft–arm angle, but lower the club head behind the ball by bending your back a little more.

Your shoulders will go down, your seat backwards, and your hands nearer your body. The upper part of your spine will become horizontal or nearly so, depending on the length of the club shaft.

If the club head is not then in the exact position with its centre behind the ball, do not adjust it with your hands or arms. Do it by shuffling your feet forwards, backwards, right or left, as required, at the same time seeing that the club shaft is at right angles to the intended line of flight.

SUMMARY

Most players, if they will only try it, will probably find it better to play every shot with a perfectly square, widish stance, with little—if any—reduction in width as the club shafts and the shots become shorter.

The feet should be placed exactly as when walking, and flat on the ground; but if found necessary, either put more weight on the heels or grip the ground with the toes.

The player must also see that he stands in correct relationship to the ball position. For all iron shots, have the ball about midway between the left heel and the centre of the stance, but a little farther to the right if you prefer to take a divot. For a drive have the ball a little—or maybe more—to the left.

By means of this standardised stance, ball position, and swing, with only the left shoulder to think about, the supposedly difficult game of golf will be greatly simplified.

All shots should—mathematically—go straight, but there may be slight variations of ball position required for players with wide shoulders, etc.

If you prove to be one for whom the open or closed stance gives better results—there may be a few such people —always see that your shoulders are square—i.e., have your left shoulder pointing to the target. And remember that with an open stance the ball should be farther to the right, and with a closed stance farther to the left, than with a square stance.

With the foregoing data in mind, let us now take up the stance and address the ball.

1. Walk to the ball, estimate the distance of the shot, and decide which club to use; then take from your bag the club which is "one stronger". That is to say, if you decide that you can do the distance with a five, use a four. This under-estimating of your ability will usually pay big dividends, since a very large percentage of shots to the green are "short".

If you cannot see the green from where your ball is, then walk forward until you can, because raised ground between you and the green usually renders the distance very deceptive—even if you can see the flag.

2. Walk back a few yards from the ball, then take the grip in the following manner: bring both shoulders forward and ground the club head, and as you do so pull your left "shoulder" upwards until you feel a distinct "hollowing" of the right side of your body, which will cause the rest of you, and the club, to assume the position of the "set". It is a good practice to get this preliminary feeling before going near the ball. Also if you took the grip without doing it, the club face would probably be open at impact unless you had adjusted the grip before swinging. From that position, then, grip the club while the club head is in the correct position relative to the stance, and the club face at the correct angle. From then *be conscious of maintaining a firm grip*.

3. Face the target and walk towards the ball, so that it is on the line between you and the target; then fix a spot with your eyes a foot or so behind the ball. As you walk

to the ball, don't stand upright, but retain some of the back-bending and "hollowed" right side, and also the angle between your arms and the club shaft, with your upper arms lightly touching your body.

4. When about to take up the stance, the club head will be near the ball but probably above it. Put your feet down in their normal walking angle, and in correct relationship to the ball, and also with the toes parallel to the line between the ball and the spot which you picked out behind it.

Meanwhile you have bent your knees, and you are more or less crouching over the ball, and looking down at the back of it.

5. If the club head is higher than the ball, lower it by bending your back. Don't do it with your hands, as that would alter the arm–club-shaft angle. The arms should be about perpendicular, and the club shaft at right angles to the intended line of flight.

6. When the club head is grounded, if it is not in quite the correct position, again, don't adjust it with your hands, as that would alter the natural position of your arms. Instead, move your feet in the appropriate direction, adjusting them at the same time for ball position and width of stance.

7. You are now nearly ready to begin the back-swing. While adjusting your feet you might glance at the target, then turn your head slightly to the right, if you need this "chin-pointing" technique.

8. Finally, give the club shaft a good squeeze with both your hands to make sure you really have a firm grip that will enable you to "hold on" at the top; and ground the club head by letting it rest on the ground close behind the ball, at the back of which you are looking; and now is the moment! Left shoulder down, left shoulder up more quickly. The shot is over!

That attempted description of the assumption of the grip, set, stance, and address took much longer than the actual performance. Also it is difficult, if not impossible, to place every item in the correct sequence, as many details which the description might suggest occur separately—in fact, occur simultaneously.

Nevertheless. it will serve as a guide to this very important part of the game; and it should be made a kind of drill, until it becomes second nature to do all these things.

Only by that method can you get the golfing machine— i.e., your body, feet, knees, hips, arms, and the club—into the correct positions for commencing the back-swing comfortably and naturally, without a lot of disjointed movements and adjustments after taking the stance.

If you have got this "foundation" for the swing correct, then you have only to concentrate on revolving your shoulders around the upper part of your spine.

It has been truly said that if the back-swing is correct, the forward swing will probably be so too. We might preface that with: "If the preparation of the foundation is correct, the back-swing has a good chance of being correct."

It will no doubt be noticed that I have not mentioned "the waggle". This is not an oversight. I thoroughly disapprove of it, for the following reasons. It is impossible to waggle with the club head at ground level except backwards and forwards up to the ball, which many players do. My objection to this procedure is that it can be done only by early wrist-bending, which is freely condemned by all. Yet there are those who say that the "waggle" fits into, or is an integral part of the back-swing. How can these two statements be reconciled? Not only must this "waggle-wrist-cocking" be too early to be part of the swing, but it must also be performed voluntarily by the hands, which, as we have seen, is not the way to swing a golf club.

The other method—of waggling to and fro above the ball—necessitates lifting the club up, either by bending the wrists or arms, or by raising the body—either of which will necessitate later, and possibly fatal, readjustments. In addition, this method—just as the other—encourages beginning the back-swing by the hands and early wrist-cocking.

It is much more important to feel that the club shaft is really being gripped; then the wrists will take care of themselves without this so-called "freeing" of them. The adjustment of the stance by shuffling the feet as described will prevent the player from becoming statuesque.

CHAPTER II

THE GRIP

THE grip may be "two-handed", in which the right hand is below and close to the left one; "interlocking", which is really the same, except that the little finger of the right hand is interlocking with the index finger of the left hand; or "overlapping", in which the little finger of the right hand overlaps the index finger of the left hand, making only seven fingers in contact with the shaft instead of eight.

The last mentioned is the one usually used and recommended, and is the only one I propose to discuss in detail. Since there are only seven fingers on the shaft, the wrists are closer together, and therefore work more in unison. To some extent this also simplifies the swing, because in my opinion *ninety per cent of golf's difficulties are due to the fact that the left hand is higher on the club shaft than the right one, but with this grip it is less high.*

To avoid becoming lost in a maze of detail, we will consider the grip under nine headings, dealing first with broad principles.

IMPORTANCE OF THE GRIP

It is impossible to over-estimate the importance of the grip.

If—as it certainly is—the swing is "half the battle", the grip is most of the other half.

The important thing in executing a golf stroke, as distinct from swinging a club, is that the club face must be square to the ball—i.e., at right angles to the target line—when it strikes the ball.

This ideal state of affairs depends almost entirely on the

grip. If either hand, or both, are placed on the club shaft turned either too much to the left or right, then the club face, instead of facing the target at impact, will be facing either right or left; and consequently the ball, instead of going towards the target, will travel either to the right or to the left. A similar result may accrue if the grip is not uniformly firm throughout the swing.

LEFT HAND SUPPORTS THE CLUB

To support the club, the left wrist must be—in part at least—on top of (i.e., above) the shaft, in a similar position to that of the right hand for a *backhand* tennis drive.

Grip the shaft with your left hand, just as you would naturally hold a whip or stick to administer a *backhand* blow. Notice your wrist partly on top of the shaft, and also how easily you can hold or swing the club.

It is supported in front by your index finger, and pushed down at the back by the heel of your hand. Prove this by turning your hand to the left so that the heel of the hand is not on top, and notice how much heavier the club feels, and how much more difficult to swing while keeping the club face at the correct angle.

RIGHT-HAND POSITION

Speaking broadly, the right hand should be behind the shaft, in a similar position to that for the tennis forehand drive—that is, with the palm approximately facing the target. Guard against the common tendency to get this hand under the shaft. If anything, the palm should be facing slightly downwards rather than upwards.

I would like to reiterate these two principles, which, although obvious, are often overlooked, and are at the same time the foundation of any good grip. They are, that *with the left arm the blow is backhanded, while with the right arm it is forehanded*; therefore the golf stroke is a combination of the two, and the grip with each hand must be appropriate to its purpose.

If the reader will experiment with a stick or any implement, with each hand separately, he will find that *by no other hold can he accurately hit a ball or other object, straight to his left.*

USE OF LEFT THUMB

I don't like a grip which does not make use of the left thumb, because it is unnatural. I have in mind the grip in which the left thumb is behind the shaft, pointing to the ground.

Try to pick up anything—much less grip it—with either hand without using your thumb. You will at once realise the importance of the thumb. Its function is to oppose a finger—in the case of golf, the index finger—when gripping. Therefore if you don't use your left thumb, neither do you use your left index finger, and the club is then held by only the last three fingers and the palm. Why weaken the grip?

Just as the heel of the left hand exerts counter pressure to assist the index finger to support the club at the address, so at the top of the back-swing should the left thumb exert counter pressure to help the little finger to support the club.

Since the thumb at the top of the swing is in some degree under the shaft, it greatly minimises the strain on the little finger. If the thumb were not there, the player would be much more likely to "let go". Also there would be nothing to check the club falling behind your back in an overswing, and no final "tightening of the spring" felt in the left wrist.

I am driven to the conclusion that however well a man may play without his left thumb, he would play better with it.

FIRM GRIP

Here are a few examples of the nonsense which I have read, and been told, about the strength of the grip.

1. Grip more tightly with the little, or fifth finger of the left hand.

2. Grip more tightly with the fourth and fifth—or the third, fourth and fifth—fingers of the left hand.

3. Grip firmly with the thumbs and index fingers of both hands, but less so than with the left little finger.

4. The whole right-hand grip is less firm than the left-hand grip.

5. The whole grip with both hands should be no stronger than that required to hold a pen or a knife and fork.

It is not possible to hit a ball and maintain any or all of these various grades of grip.

The light grip which is so frequently taught is the cause of so many people "letting go" at the top of the back-swing. I believe it is also the cause of the blister which ultimately becomes a callous (i.e., hard skin) which frequently develops in the left palm just above the little finger. Some people think the callous is caused by movement of the club shaft in the hand—which movement is, of course, due to not gripping tightly enough. I am sure they are right, because it is a fact that callouses and corns on people's feet are caused by intermittent pressure.

If you think of any homely incident such as killing a rat with a stick, or driving a stake into the ground with a mallet, you would not think of varying the pressure with different fingers, or of a tight grip. With the intention to hit hard, you would grip "hard".

It has been said that the grip automatically tightens at impact, by which time the club may be held as in a vice. I don't believe it! Are we to believe that it is owing to this automatic vice-like grip that so many people let the club shaft turn in the hands at impact? On the contrary, I think that if the club is lightly gripped at address it is much more likely to become looser at impact, which belief is supported by the two common faults of "letting go" at the top and letting the club shaft turn in the hands at impact.

There might be some excuse for the lighter grip for a "lighter" shot, say a half shot or a chip or a putt; but even with these shots you are told to strike the ball firmly— and I agree—but how can you strike firmly with a light or loose grip? I am sure that this teaching is responsible for so much poor play "around the green".

I believe those good players who think they start with a light grip tighten the grip—maybe subconsciously— immediately before they start the back-swing. Surely the intention to hit exists from that moment!

Also, remember that after you have taken a really firm grip your mind will be concentrated on the swing and hitting the ball; and that your difficulty will be to maintain that grip throughout the swing, with your mind otherwise occupied.

You need a really tight grip to hold on at the top—as everybody in authority agrees you should do. Also, all are agreed that you should be gripping with all your might at impact; otherwise you could not get that recommended, and much-desired, "solid contact" with the ball without which it could not go a long way.

Nowadays—I am glad to notice—more amd more professionals are advocating a firm or very firm grip; and although only some of them say from the address, that is what they all mean, if I interpret their phraseology correctly.

Some—the ones with whom I most heartily agree—say grip very firmly with both hands, while others split hairs by saying "firm" but not "tight". Surely those are synonymous terms!

Others say—in effect—that if you fail to hit a number of balls in succession correctly without adjusting the grip, then it was not firm enough. Now, if, as some experts teach, the grip is relaxed at address and tight at impact, we should have to relax the grip for each successive shot. It must be obvious that these frequent changes of muscular intensity would allow—if not cause—some alteration of the grip position. I am quite certain that to perform this feat you would require a really tight grip with all parts of both hands. I am no less certain that that should be the attitude regarding the grip for all shots—i.e., as firm, or tight, as necessary.

Having defeated Henry Cotton, Flory van Donck, and Jimmy Adams to win the 1951 *News of the World* Golf Tournament, Harry Weetman was reputed to be a much-improved player since returning to golf after having been employed felling trees with a seven-pound axe; and to have acquired (presumably in consequence) a vice-like grip.

I know that some readers—despite the authoritative support for my contention—will be thinking: "What about the wrists?" It is only necessary to grip a club really firmly with both hands and to swing, to convince yourself that firm gripping does not interfere with necessary wrist work—and if you swing at a ball, the "solid contact" will astonish you.

I have proved to my satisfaction that the wrists will function efficiently—and automatically—no matter how tightly you grip the club shaft, providing you concentrate on your left shoulder for the whole swing, back and forward.

If you do that, then centrifugal force—plus maybe some subconscious help from you—will swing the arms across, and undo any wrist-cocking at the correct time and place.

Finally I will demonstrate an anatomical fact which influences the grip, and which the reader can prove for himself. The bones of our fingers and hands are covered with compressible flesh. From the start you must compress that flesh, and grip with the bones. It is a case of "the nearer the bone, the sweeter the shot". Some people's hands swell during the early morning or in hot weather. In those circumstances they will play better golf if they grip more firmly than usual so as to compress that "additional cushion".

Now for proof: address a ball using the usual light grip, watch the club face and forcibly tighten the grip. I think you will find that the angle of the club face has changed—probably "opened". It certainly will if you tighten the grip of only one hand or part of it—which is further evidence in favour of gripping firmly with all parts of both hands, all the time.

I would implore the reader not to dismiss my arguments, and all the evidence I have cited, with the one word "tension". It has been observed that an angry golfer might play better in consequence of his anger. The only thing anger could do would be to increase his tension—and concentration—and make him grip more fiercely.

THICKNESS OF CLUB-SHAFT HANDLE

I will first of all disprove the belief that short fingers necessitate thin grips. If a child, say ten years of age, plays tennis he uses a junior racket, the oblong handle of which is equivalent to a diameter of one and one-eighth of an inch. At about the age of fourteen years he uses a full-size racket with handle equivalent to one and a half inches diameter. Even the thinner tennis-racket handle is thick compared with even the thickest—much less the average—golf-club handle.

All other implements for playing games—even table

tennis—are thick handled, so why use a puny golf-club grip?

I have experimented with all thicknesses of grip, from the bare steel shaft with only a leather "grip"—which was very uncomfortable—to grips of one and a quarter inches in diameter.

I prefer, and would recommend, for all clubs—including the putter—a shaft built up to seven-eighths of an inch diameter from top to bottom of the grip, without any tapering.

Tapering of the grip I believe to be unnecessary, and in fact undesirable, because if you have to grip "down the stick", the grip and the shot feel different. This surely makes the game more complicated without any corresponding advantage.

The grip can be taken with greater mathematical accuracy for all shots if the handle is the same thickness throughout. What proves best for some experts—and myself—may also be so for many others.

Golf-club handles used to be made the same thickness throughout, but it seems that when the necessity for a thicker handle became apparent manufacturers made the mistake of thickening only the end under the left hand for a full shot—hence the tapering. But this desirable thickness often protrudes beyond the left hand, and therefore is not utilised. Surely if it is considered desirable at all—which it is—then the thickness should be where it will always be used—that is, throughout.

Even though the top part of many golf-club handles is somewhat thickened, some professionals recommend further thickening under the left hand to "assist holding on"; and some wear a left-hand glove, ostensibly to aid gripping, but which—in effect—makes the handle thicker, which is probably the real advantage.

The best way to convince yourself of the undesirability

of a thin grip is to use the thinnest possible one. You will then realise the inherent disadvantages of any thin grip, which are not so apparent when it is only moderately thin, and especially if you have no experience of thick grips as a comparison.

Thin handles must be held too much in the fingers, therefore the grip—and the blow—lack power. Also they give the wrists too much play, thereby encouraging too much wrist-cocking at the top, and over-swinging, instead of the modern restricted wrist-cock and compact back-swing.

Similar ill effects occur at impact where, instead of "solid contact", you tend to get a wrist-flick owing to lack of sufficient "something" to hold on to.

The acid test is, can you "hold on"? Prove for yourself how much more firmly you can grip a rod one inch in diameter, than one which is half as thick.

ELEMENTARY ANATOMY OF THE ARM AND HAND

We must now study the construction and function of the arm, hand, and fingers; and give the various parts simple names, so that it is clear to which parts we refer.

All joints are made to function by muscles, which are attached to bone above and below the joint. When the muscle "contracts"—that is, becomes hard, firm, tight, taut, or tense—it also becomes shorter, therefore it brings together the two bones to which it is attached, the inter-vening joint acting as a hinge.

(A) **The Shoulder Joint.** This is called a ball-and-socket joint, which therefore is capable of movement in any direction including a circular movement. Use of this joint moves the upper arm.

(B) **The Elbow Joint.** This is a hinge joint, which there-fore moves only in one plane. The "hinge" can be "closed" by bringing the hand towards the shoulder; and "opened" by straightening the arm, in which position it "locks" when fully extended. Use of the elbow joint moves the forearm. Note that any upward straying of the right "elbow" on the back-swing is performed by the shoulder joint raising the upper arm. Therefore this fault is caused either by commencing the back-swing with the right arm, or by the right arm being pushed upwards owing to the right hand being "under" the shaft.

(C) **The Forearm Bones.** The forearm contains two long bones (the radius and ulna), the ends of which form the elbow and wrist joints. When you turn your hand palm upwards it is supine—that is, you have supinated your hand. In this position the forearm bones lie parallel. When you turn your hand palm downwards, it is prone—that is, you have pronated your hand. In this position one forearm bone lies across the other—just like "crossed fingers". I have explained these actions because I have seen them wrongly described in golf books under the one term "pronation". In the golf swing, when one hand pronates, the other must supinate; but actually there is very little of this movement in the correct golf swing, the greatest part being towards the end of the forward swing when the right hand climbs over the left.

This is the so-called wrist-roll, which many people describe as occurring before, or soon after impact. Really this is largely an optical illusion, and is due to the fact that as the hands pass from right to left, so do the shoulders turn; so that the hands are always more or less "in front of" the upper part of the body.

In any case the golfer has no concern with the movement. If and when it does occur, it does so automatically, and secondarily to the swing of the arms caused by the revolving shoulders.

(D) **The Wrist Joint.** The simplest description of this is "a complex hinge joint". There are four main movements, and also four combinations of any two adjacent movements:

1. Back of the hand towards forearm—about 45 degrees.
2. Palm of the hand towards forearm—about 80 degrees.
3. Little finger side of the hand towards forearm—about 50 degrees.
4. Thumb side of hand towards forearm—about 10 degrees.
5. The only combination movement in which we are interested is of numbers one and four. To affect that, you bring the index finger knuckle back towards the junction of the thumb side and the back of the forearm.

That movement is the automatic wrist-cocking which occurs on the back-swing and in the average wrist is probably not more than twenty degrees beyond the grip position at address. The important point is that that small amount of involuntary wrist movement produces a movement of the club head of maybe three feet. That is why I say that at the top of the back-swing your sensation should be that the club shaft is approximately pointing to the sky; then with little, if any, further upward movement of your hands, this very small automatic wrist movement will swing the club head to something approaching the horizontal, while you are beginning the forward swing with your left shoulder.

(E) **The Hand.** See Diagram No. 4. Near the wrist we have two bulges in the palm of the hand, which we will call the "heel of the hand" and the "ball of the thumb". Running upwards from the wrist between these two bulges is a groove in which lies the "life-line" of palmistry. To see these bulges and the groove clearly, bring together the tips of your thumb and little finger.

Another important point about the hand is that the

fingers are about one inch longer than they appear to be when you look at the palm of your hand. Their full length is measured from the knuckles seen on the back of the hand. Note also the "palmistry line" across the palm, which indicates the position of the knuckles.

Running from the knuckles to the wrist are the meta-carpal bones—one from each finger. We are greatly interested in the one from the little finger of the left hand. If the reader will apply his right thumb to the "heel" of his left hand he will feel the large bulbous end of the metacarpal bone. That is the portion of the left hand which should be on top of the club shaft when it is gripped.

The hand—through the wrist joint—is moved by muscles in the forearm.

(F) **The Fingers.** See Diagram No. 4. Counting from what look like the bases of the fingers when seen in the palm, each finger is divided into three segments, which we will call the first, second, and third segments of the fingers. Each finger has also three creases, which we will call the first, second, and third creases of the fingers. Note that the second crease marks the position of what we will call the *finger* knuckle, in contradistinction to the knuckle proper.

The fingers are moved partly by small muscles in the hand, but chiefly by muscles in the forearm with long tendons going down to the fingers.

(G) **The Thumb.** See Diagram No. 4. The thumb has only two creases and two segments.

It is important to notice the shape of the thumb. When gripping a golf club, the second segment should be bent right back—that is to say, it should be "straightened" or fully extended. With the thumb in that position, pressure is applied to the club shaft by the middle of the second segment (opposite the base of the nail), and not by the tip of the thumb.

DETAILS OF THE GRIP

For the purpose of accurate description, it will be well to visualise the club shaft as being square on cross section. I will accordingly speak of four surfaces and four "corners".

The surfaces are the top, bottom or under, left or front, and right or back.

The corners are the top left, top right, bottom left, and bottom right.

The anatomical parts to which I will refer are: the heel of the hand and the bulbous end of the metacarpal bone "inside" it, the ball of the thumb, the groove between the two bulges, the knuckle proper, the finger knuckle, the segments and creases of the fingers and thumbs by number, the base of the thumb nail, and the callous which forms in the palm just above the base of the little finger.

We are now in possession of all the data necessary to study intelligently the method of taking the grip. I will describe only that which I recommend for all clubs, from the driver to the putter—namely, the overlapping grip, which is said to have been originated by the late Harry Vardon.

While the great majority of professionals use this grip, they apparently have different conceptions of the relationship of the fingers and palm to the club shaft, according to the descriptions and pictures in their books. Hitherto there has been no explanation offered to account for the need for these variations. I will endeavour to supply it.

The grip should be taken with mathematical accuracy, since it is the means of bringing the club face to the ball exactly at right angles to the target line.

The grip is usually described as a finger grip, a palm grip, or a combination of both; but as a matter of fact there is no such thing as a palm grip in golf. The only thing the palm is capable of gripping is a coin placed in its centre, as practised by conjurors.

I am not quibbling over the established nomenclature for quibbling's sake. These inaccurate descriptions definitely confuse people. The grip worried me for years— as I know it does others—and I am sure that half the trouble is due to variations in the descriptions offered, without any adequate explanation as to their necessity. I hope to get rid of that confusion.

Actually there are only two possible methods of gripping a golf club—but with various degrees of obliquity in each.

There is the finger-grip, in which the fingers entwine round the shaft; this is assisted by the apposition of the thumb.

With a really thin shaft, this grip is almost inevitable, because the "handle" is too small to fill the hand, and therefore a hand grip would not be firm enough. That statement—the truth of which is obvious—is quite sufficient to condemn thin handles.

The other and better method is the hand grip, in which the whole hand is used—that is to say, all the anatomy from the wrist to the finger-tips.

If we were going to grip an article—say, a golf ball—we would hold it in the hand, "make a fist", and squeeze. Now, if in place of the ball we put the handle of a golf club and grip in the same manner, then the club shaft will be at right angles to the forearm.

If the reader will now do that with his left hand, and examine his hand, he will see that this hand grip is four-sided.

On the under surface are the top ends of the fingers where they join the palm; on the right side are the "nail-ends" of the fingers; on the left side, the palm; and on the top, the heel of the hand and the ball of the thumb.

It is obvious that by gripping a golf club in that manner

we could not hit a golf ball that was on the ground, therefore some degree of obliquity of the grip becomes necessary.

For that reason the "front portion" of the grip must, to some extent, be held by the index finger and thumb, because if we allow the grip to become oblique, then the thumb itself either takes the place of or reinforces the ball of the thumb —which, it will be remembered, was on top of the shaft.

It will be realised that the farther the shaft is allowed to go "down" the index finger and thumb, the more obliquely will it be lying across the hand.

This *variation in obliquity* will cause slight variations in the relationship of the club handle to the different parts of the hand and fingers, and is the explanation of the varying descriptions offered in different golf books.

The difference in obliquity will depend on several factors, such as different build of players, especially their height and length of arms; also different lengths of club shaft used by people of similar build. For example, if a player uses clubs that are too long for him—as many people do—and wishes to bend the upper part of his back as the professionals do, then he will have to use a grip with only a little obliquity. On the other hand, if he has cultivated a grip with considerable obliquity, then he will have to stand too upright.

From this truth—which cannot be gainsaid—it becomes obvious that a proper grip cannot be acquired unless the golf clubs are short enough to "fit" the player.

Let us for a moment consider the function of the hand and fingers and prove which is the better method of gripping a golf club. First of all, a hand without a thumb would be relatively useless. The finger-tips in conjunction with the thumb-tip are used for very delicate work, such as needle-threading and watch-repairing. The entire finger and thumb are used for work less fine, such as holding a pen or a glass of wine. For heavier work, such as holding a

tankard of beer, a tennis racket, or a golf club—or anything of similar weight—the whole hand should be used.

Now, since it is established that when a player grips a
golf club, the sole function of the hands is to become part
of the club—the wrists acting merely as hinges—and that
the grip must be firm and immovable, it is surely obvious
that the grip must be made with the strongest part of the
anatomy possible. That part is the entire hand, so hence-
forth let us forget all about finger and palm grips, and—
with whatever degree of obliquity we find necessary—
simply think of gripping a golf club, with the hands.

I am not alone in advocating a hand grip. I believe most
professionals do, but they wrongly describe it as a palm
grip, or a combination of palm and finger grip, apparently forgetting that when the hand is "closed" the handle
must be in the hand. In addition, there are numerous
photographs in most golf books that show clearly that the
club handle is gripped by the entire left hand.

This is most readily seen to be beyond doubt at the top
of the back-swing, viewed from "behind the shot".

Different descriptions of finger, palm, or hand grip
usually refer in particular to the left hand, but the right-
hand grip is no less important. Most professionals state
that they grip only with the fingers of the right hand.
While it is true that only their fingers and thumb are in
contact with the club, I maintain that they nevertheless
grip *something* with the entire hand. Nearly everybody
appears to have overlooked the fact that the right hand,
between the top part of the palm and the little finger, grips
the left index-finger and thumb, with the shaft in between
them. Because this fact is apparently overlooked and
never sufficiently mentioned, lots of players don't do it
efficiently. I will only ask the reader how the entire grip
can be made immovable—as it should be—if the right hand
is not fixed to the left one by gripping it as described?

If the player will grip in the manner described he will be conscious of using the entire right hand as well as the entire left hand, and his hands will definitely become merely "a part of the shaft", thus conforming to professional requirements.

I will now describe in detail the relationship of the hand and fingers to the club-shaft handle. In my view, the most natural, most comfortable, and most powerful hand grip— for most people—is one in which the club shaft lies across the left hand at an angle of almost exactly forty-five degrees.

Left Hand. If the reader will again examine Diagram No. 4, he will see a line "A–B" which represents the centre of the club shaft, passing obliquely across the hand. On the little finger side of the palm it will be seen that this line exactly bisects the palm between the base of the little finger (first crease) and the "wrist crease"; while on the other side of the hand it crosses over the centre of the second crease of the index finger. That line "A–B" should be applied to the club-shaft handle when taking the left-hand grip.

The surface of the club shaft to which this line should be applied will vary slightly with the size of hand and thickness of handle, because the relative positions of the index finger and thumb on top of the handle when the hand is "closed" must not vary.

With an average hand and thickish club handle, the left hand should be placed with its surface perpendicular, on the front, or left, surface of the club shaft. By thus accurately placing your left hand, you will have taken the most important step in assuming a good, firm, and natural left-hand grip.

Keeping that position quite definite, simply "close" the fingers, and "wrap" the palm to the right over the handle, and everything will fit in. The heel of the hand, containing the thick end of the metacarpal bone, will come down on top of the handle, and the thumb will be applied to the "top right corner". The tip of the thumb will be about a quarter of an inch farther down the shaft than the index finger, therefore the middle of the "second segment" of the thumb (opposite the base of the nail) will be directly opposite the "second segment" of the index finger, the centre of the shaft being compressed between them.

The above-described relationship between the left thumb and left index finger has been named the "low thumb" (or "long thumb") left-hand grip. N.B. It is significant that golf professional W. J. Cox reported that during a Ryder Cup Match many years ago most of the victorious American team *used this grip*. So it appears that I am in good company; and also that by taking my advice you will be emulating these world beaters!

The reader will recall my discussion on variations in obliquity of grip, and will therefore know that this "winning grip" is possible only if the player uses clubs short enough to "fit" him when the *upper* part of his back is well bent. (For further details of this subject, read "The Golf Secret".)

I have intentionally omitted one detail, so as to emphasise its importance. You will remember that the bones of your fingers and hand are covered with compressible flesh. It will be apparent that, having assumed the above grip, there will be this cushion—like a pneumatic tyre—between the bones and the club shaft, therefore any uneven pressure will alter the position of the club shaft, and consequently the angle of the club face.

This we must avoid as follows:

With the club head flat on the ground, hold the end of the shaft with the right index finger and thumb, then, having placed the left hand in its correct position on the front of the handle, press it hard against the handle as you close your fingers and the hand, thus compressing the flesh. Finally, grip the handle very firmly with the whole of the left hand and fingers, pushing the heel of the hand downwards.

Inspection of the "outside" of the hand will show that the finger-knuckle of the index finger and part of the back of the hand are both directly to the front of the left side of the handle. It is usually said that the back of the left hand faces the target—another of the many inaccuracies that have been glibly offered to would-be golfers! If that were true, you would be able to see only one knuckle, instead of two or three. With the hand correctly placed on the shaft, it is only the "lower half" of the back of the hand which faces the target, while the "upper half" is curved to face somewhat skywards.

If you look directly down at your hand, you will see the wrist on top of the shaft, and an equal amount of "hand" on each side of the shaft. You will also see the first two knuckles very prominently, and will probably just see the third one.

Finally, the left-most edge of the thumb marks the dead centre of the shaft, while the groove between the thumb and the hand (often mistakenly called the "vee") will be pointing more or less towards the right shoulder, depending on how wide your shoulders are.

Right Hand. Maintaining the left-hand grip as above described, now apply the right hand perpendicularly to the back, or right surface of the handle, so that when the hand is "closed", the left thumb is completely out of sight, and resting in the "groove" of the right palm.

Close the fingers round the handle, so that the little finger is resting on top of the left index finger; and if necessary draw the right hand upwards until the third or ring finger is very close to the left index finger.

Adjust the right index finger if necessary so that its

"second segment" is under the shaft and parallel to the ground. The first segment of this finger will then be behind the shaft, although it will appear to encroach on top because the soft flesh bulges in that direction, especially when you press your right hand—as you should—against the back of the shaft and the left thumb, so as to compress the flesh and grip with the bones.

The right thumb should be lying across the "top left corner" of the handle, and pointing to the left and downwards at an angle of about forty-five degrees. The right thumb points in this direction because the right palm is separated from the shaft by the left thumb. For the same reason the right thumb opposes the right index finger rather differently than in the case of the left hand. The left thumb compresses the shaft against the second segment of the index finger, while the right thumb compresses the shaft against the second crease of the index finger.

The little finger, which we left resting on top of the left index finger, should be adjusted to suit your own comfort. The position will vary with length of fingers and thickness of club handle. It may remain resting on the second segment of the index finger or "farther on", gripping the "finger knuckle"; or it may rest or grip in the groove between the left index and middle fingers.

Now, notice that between the "wrist end" of the palm of your right hand and the right little finger you are holding your left index finger and thumb with the shaft in between them. Whatever position you have chosen for your right little finger, I would strongly recommend that you really grip everything that lies between that finger and the palm of the right hand. Only by so doing can you with certainty make both of your hands become immovably part of the shaft. Those who advocate the interlocking grip claim that its superiority is due to this locking together of the hands by the little finger being firmly anchored;

so let us have this advantage along with the more natural, and more comfortable, overlapping grip.

Finally, the remaining two fingers (ring and middle) are opposing the palm in gripping the shaft.

Inspection of the "outside" of the hand will show the trigger-like position of the index finger, and the tip of the thumb somewhat higher on the shaft. (Whereas the left thumb tip was lower than the index finger.) Also, the wrist and back of the hand are behind the shaft, so that you can see only two knuckles, the second of which is not prominent. The groove between the thumb and the hand points in the direction of the right shoulder, but maybe slightly less so than in the case of the left hand.

You have now assumed an orthodox overlapping grip—but with a difference. The difference being that you have utilised—and intend to use—every part of both hands. If you really grip that club shaft very firmly, then wild horses could not take the club from you, let alone the golf swing making you "let go".

Wrists. A description of the golf grip would be incomplete without some reference to the wrists in relation to it. With the grip above described, the wrists are automatically placed in the best position to allow them to work together—i.e., almost as one.

The wrists are usually described as being close together, which simply means that they are not one on either side of the shaft. The left wrist is on top of the shaft, the forearm running slightly to the left, thus forming an angle with the back of the hand. The right wrist is an inch or two behind the shaft, and two or three inches nearer the ground than the left one, because the right hand is farther down the shaft. The right forearm runs to the right in a line almost continuous with the back of the hand, therefore there is little or no angle at the wrist.

We will now demonstrate the influence of the grip on

wrist-cocking. Assume the grip and address a ball, then, by means of the hands only, bring the club head straight up towards your face. Notice how that grip permits the two wrists to function together. As a contrast, maintain the left-hand grip, but turn the right hand in its entirety, say, half an inch to the right. Now try to cock the wrists by bringing the club head towards your face, and notice how they work unevenly and against each other.

That little demonstration should settle your desire— once and for all—of wanting to get your right hand "under" the shaft; which fault, in addition to tending to shut the club face at impact, tends to obstruct the back-swing, and thus cause the right elbow to assume a high position.

On the other hand, with the right hand in the correct position, the back-swing is performed without hindrance, the right elbow stays low down, and wrist-cocking becomes natural and easy, because the wrists are in the position which allows them both to bend in the same direction.

INDIVIDUAL ADJUSTMENTS OF THE GRIP

Once you have grasped all the details of the grip as described, don't readily change any portion of it. I believe it will produce the best results for most people.

See what happens when you play a lot of shots. If the ball travels mostly in a straight line and with the correct trajectory, then all is well. On the other hand, if it persistently goes to the right or left, there are several possible causes for that, apart from the grip. I will list them and suggest remedies.

1. You may not be gripping tightly enough with *both* hands, and consequently letting go at the top, over-swinging, allowing the club to turn in your hands at impact, or not making "solid contact".

2. Maybe you forgot to bend your back to get your

arms about perpendicular, or maybe your club shaft is too long to allow it; consequently you may be swinging too flat. Put your hands two inches farther "down the stick", and look down at the ball.

3. Maybe your left shoulder is not going down enough on the back-swing, and in consequence your shoulder pivot is incomplete, causing an outside-to-in forward swing.

4. Maybe your left shoulder is not going up enough on the forward swing, in which case you might pull the ball to the left, or slice it.

5. You may be swaying, but this is not likely if your left shoulder is going down and up correctly.

6. You may be lifting your head, but this is unlikely if your back is correctly bent and your left shoulder is moving properly.

7. You may not be swinging freely enough, but instead, trying to guide the club. Think of stone-throwing, and take your left shoulder up as quickly as possible on the forward swing.

8. By using hands or arms you may be snatching. Think only of your left shoulder, and try making a definite—though momentary—stop at the top of the back-swing.

9. Though not snatching, maybe the arms are getting into the shot before the body. Stop at the top and think only of your left shoulder.

10. You may be addressing the ball with the club face slightly open or shut. It is quite common to think the face is square when it is not. Get a friend to check it. He might see what you cannot.

11. You may have the ball a little too far to the right or left for *you*. A common cause of having the ball too far to the right, is having the left shoulder too low at address owing to not adopting the correct "set". Check up on the set, then try slight variations of ball position.

12. You may not be standing as you think you are.

Address a ball in what you think to be a square stance, then lay the club across your toes, go behind the shot, and see where the club is pointing.

13. Having tried out all the above possibilities, if the ball still refuses to go "straight down the middle", you should alter the position of your hands on the club, because a slight variation will no doubt be necessary owing to differences of build, shoulder width, length of arms, etc. Except as a last resort, don't change the position of one hand relative to the other.

If the ball goes frequently to the right, then turn both your hands, in their entirety, one-eighth of an inch to the right. If the ball still travels to the right, turn your hands another eighth of an inch to the right, and so on—only a fraction at a time—until the ball goes straight.

If the ball goes frequently to the left, then turn both hands in their entirety one-eighth of an inch to the left, very gradually increasing the amount of hand-turn until you repeatedly hit the ball straight to the target.

14. Finally, if you still cannot hit a consistently straight ball, it is probable that you are one of those people who are a "law unto themselves". If so, do not be dejected, as there are quite a few among the experts who grip differently from the majority, by placing either one hand or the other more to the right or left.

If, then, you are in this category, you will have to find by experiment the relative positions of the two hands to suit you. You will probably have to either cover still more of your left thumb by turning the right hand to the left or the left hand to the right; or expose more of your left thumb by turning the right hand to the right or the left hand to the left.

The final adjustment from either of the above positions will be to turn both hands together either to the left or right, depending on the direction taken by the ball.

CHAPTER III

THE PUTT, THE CHIP-SHOT, AND THE STYMIE

I WILL discuss the putt, the chip-shot, and the stymie together, because I think they are best thought of as the
same shot played with different clubs; which in fact they
are, or at least may be, and I believe—preferably—should
be.

Further, they are really no different from other golf
shots, except that they are "part shots", the whole swing
taking place in the lower—or middle—portions of the
swing arc. It should be recalled that the bottom of the arc
is automatically flattened.

These being short shots and essentially in slow tempo,
certain modifications of preparation and execution become
desirable. These modifications—which should be as few
as possible—are probably the cause of players regarding
these as different from ordinary shots.

For example, at the "top of the back-swing" the player
is already in what is called the hitting area. This is the
part of the swing wherein the right arm comes into the
shot either automatically, or maybe intentionally. For
that reason they are often erroneously regarded as right-
handed shots. True, the right hand will not do so much
harm as on a full shot, but it should still be subservient to
the left side of the body. We will consider this in more
detail when discussing "the swing" for these shots.

Even among the best players there are numerous grips,
stances, attitudes, and swings used for putting. The fact is
that it is possible to putt with almost any grip or stance,
because the shot can—and should—be played by instinct
for distance, and by "eye" for line. This was forcibly

brought home to me some ten years ago, when the son of
a friend called at my house when on school holidays. To
entertain him, I suggested clock golf in my back garden.
He had never before handled a golf club, and put his left
hand below the right. I corrected this, and he proceeded
to do the nine holes in sixteen, while I took nineteen! I
am sure this was more than novice's luck: it was natural
"eye" and instinct, untrammelled by uncertainty and fear.

There are two aspects to every putt, chip-shot, or stymie:
the distance or "strength", and the direction or "line".
Most of the fuss in putting is over the "line", but in fact
the "strength" is much more important.

Golfers of all shades of ability can be seen on the greens,
performing all sorts of antics in an effort to get the correct
line, then, assuming a strained, unusual, or unnatural
grip, or some weird stance, maybe with elbows sticking out
—alternately looking up and down at the hole and the
ball, and finally often entirely misjudging the all important
"strength"—and maybe also the "line"—so that the ball
finishes a long way short of, or past, the hole, leaving a
difficult second putt, with the likelihood of a third. What
a spectacle! What an unnecessary spectacle!! I hope to
convince the reader that he will do better without all this
preparation and care.

Since the line has to be "sighted", it is much more
subject to the human element of error than the "strength",
which is more or less instinctive, if treated in that way.
For instance, if any man attempted to throw a stone either
five, ten, twenty, or thirty feet, he would probably usually
succeed within a foot or so. Again, how does a bowler so
frequently make his "wood" stop so near the "jack"?
Instinct is the only explanation. Similarly, a golfer can
usually instinctively putt a golf ball the requisite distance
merely by looking at the target and thinking of it.

Regarding the "line", I have found that it pays

handsomely to visualise a trench two feet long, and to take casual aim at the middle of it (which is the hole), and to concentrate on the strength of the blow. The ball will rarely finish as much as a foot short of, beyond, or on one side of the hole, and will often "drop in".

It pays not to be timid, because, as with approach shots to the green, if you pass the green you have had a chance to be on; similarly with putting, if you pass the hole you have had a chance to be in.

By this—carefree if not careless—method, then, if the ball does not drop, the second putt will probably be easy.

While I consider the "strength" much more important than the "line", it is nevertheless desirable to have some definite—though simple and straightforward—method by which you can depend on the ball travelling on the line which you intend. That will be provided under the headings of grip, stance, ball position, address, and the swing.

THE GRIP FOR THE THREE SHOTS

Apart from the positions of individual fingers often recommended for putting—and sometimes for chip shots —such as, index finger down the shaft, thumb-nail sticking into the leather, etc., the most generally used grip has the right hand turned a little more to the right on the shaft, and the left hand considerably more to the left.

This arrangement of the hands means that if—during the swing—the left hand assumes its natural position, then at impact the club face will be facing right and the ball will go in that direction; and if the right hand does so, then the club face at impact will be facing left and the ball will go to the left of the hole. Now, this is exactly what does happen if—as often occurs—either hand tends to overpower the other. And yet, many experts claim that the shot should be right-handed, and to enable it to be so use the reverse overlapping grip, with the left index finger over the right little finger. At the same time some of them advocate a loose grip, which surely encourages the right hand—in this position—to overpower the loosely gripping left hand, and so "shutting" the club face at impact. Frequently also, an entirely hand shot is advocated, which makes a pull to the left even more likely.

Similarly, those who grip lightly and make the shot a left-handed one are liable to have the face open at impact, and therefore to push the ball to the right owing to the left hand turning to its more natural position.

Of course I know that these hand positions are supposed to *prevent* the club face opening on the back-swing and shutting on the forward swing. But, as pointed out above, it is questionable whether they do so, as it is also questionable whether that is even desirable.

Some players try to augment this grip, or to offset its natural tendencies, by pointing one or both elbows on the target line. This is a lot of unnecessary fuss. It is a case of adopting an unsuitable grip, and then making various adjustments, in the hope that they will prevent the said grip from doing that which it is designed to do.

In my opinion—formed from experience—the ordinary straightforward overlapping grip with the hands in their normal positions is the best, and produces the most consistent results, in playing the putt, the chip-shot, and the stymie—just as it is, and does, for all other shots.

I know it is claimed that this left-handed grip used for putting encourages pulling the ball to the left, but that is definitely not so, if the swing is performed naturally in the manner later to be described.

The handle of the putter or other club used should be the same thickness as all the other clubs—that is, thickish; and also of uniform thickness throughout, without any tapering, so that the grip feels—and is—mathematically the same, whether held high or low on the shaft.

Other things being equal, it is usually better to have the hands fairly low down on the shaft, as this increases control and makes the swing more upright, because the back must then be more bent. The consequent more upright swing lessens the amount of face opening on the backswing and face shutting on the forward swing; and, even more important, it keeps the club head swinging in a straighter line, without the need for peculiar grips as artificial aids.

Players have attempted to get this straight-line shot by using a putter with a very upright lie, or by using the Vaile grip which has the shaft running the length of the hand. My objection to the former is that it causes the wrists to be arched forward into an unnatural position; and to the latter, that it is different grip with a different feel, and therefore encourages a different swing. I much prefer to have the wrists in the natural position, as with all other golf shots.

The power of the grip should be not only very firm with the left hand, but uniformly very firm with all parts of both hands. Remember that the wrists will function as much as they should, automatically, even if the grip is really tight, just as they will with full shots. For those who refuse to be persuaded of this and who insist on using a lighter grip, I will only say let the grip be of uniform power with all parts of both hands.

Briefly, then, the grip which I prefer is identical in all respects to that for all other shots.

THE STANCE FOR THE THREE SHOTS

For putting in particular, every conceivable foot position is used; and some, no doubt, are necessary to counteract the effects of a wrong grip or a faulty swing. As previously stated, a straight shot can be played from almost any stance, so long as the "shoulder stance" is approxi-

mately square. At the same time there is a "best stance",
which will assist in producing the most consistent results,
providing the other details of the shot are in keeping.

There is one small detail in the stance which I have not
yet mentioned, because we were not concerned with it until
now. If the reader will grip his putter, assume a square
stance in front of a mirror, then stand erect holding the
putter in the same relative position, he will see that his left
shoulder is higher than the right one, which is due to the
left hand being higher on the shaft, making the left arm—
in effect—longer than the right one. Now, if he bends his
back well forward to putt, his left shoulder will be somewhat nearer the target line than the right one.

This "forward position" of the left shoulder is probably
a factor in the production of the normal inside-to-out
swing in any golf shot, even though it is, at the address,
brought slightly back by the assumption of "the set".

Now, the assumption of the set on a very short shot such
as a putt would encourage too long a back-swing, neces-
sitated by the straightening of the bent right leg at the
knee. For that reason, for the shots now being considered,
instead of bringing your putter round to the ball position
by means of "the set", it is better to do so by drawing the
left foot backwards into an open stance. This will at the
same time bring the left shoulder backwards to make the
"shoulder stance" square, which position will tend more to
produce a dead straight-line shot, which is all to the good,
since an inside-to-out swing is not desirable for the short
shots we are now discussing.

Incidentally, many players—in addition to an open-foot
stance—use an open "shoulder stance", but I am sure that
that is undesirable and encourages the swing, and the ball,
to go to the left.

While it will require only a very slightly open stance to
make the shoulders square, nevertheless I have found it

better to open the foot stance considerably, but to be sure
to turn the shoulders back to the right, so that they are
square. This has the effect of causing a slight bend at the
left knee, while the left hip is held "out of the way", and the
whole left side of the body is somewhat stretched, or taut,
thus preventing too long a back-swing and also any
tendency to swing too much inside the line on the back-
swing.

This may seem complicated, but it really is not, as the
reader will see if he refers to Diagram No. 5, which represents the stance of feet and shoulders and also the position
of the club head, as seen from above.

The right foot should be put down at right angles to the
intended line of flight and parallel to the club face. With
average "angled" feet, the left foot will be at an angle of
about forty-five degrees to the right one and drawn back
from the square stance line about five inches—i.e., the left
toe will be opposite the middle of the right foot.

Regarding the distance between the feet, that will be a
matter for personal comfort, but I can see no advantage—
rather the opposite—in a very narrow stance. The
measurement is best made between the heels, which I prefer to be at least nine or ten inches apart.

If the body is correctly placed—remember the square
"shoulder stance"—then the club head will feel, and also
appear to be, nearer to the right foot than the left—which,
please note, is due to the open stance—but a line continued
backwards from the club head will pass exactly midway
between the heels. In other words, your head will be
directly over the club head, which will be at the exact
bottom of the arc, since there will be no movement of the
arc to the left by the impetus of such a short swing. The
club shaft will, of course, be at right angles to the intended
line of flight.

These three shots, then, are the only straightforward ones

for which an open stance is preferable to a square one, and that is chiefly because it does the job of the set better than the set can do it for these short shots.

I will just mention that although I have recommended a square stance for all other shots, it is just possible that some players will prefer the above described "open putting stance" for the shorter of the "part shots"—i.e., those that are little more than a chip-shot. For those who do so, I would advise regarding this not as an open stance, but merely as "the set" for short shots. They will then more easily remember the details, and not drift into the errors and faults associated with an open stance.

BALL POSITION FOR THE THREE SHOTS

Since we now know exactly where the club head should be, it is obvious that the ball should be just in front of that, but it is necessary to say a little more than that about it.

The ball position is usually very confusedly spoken of in relationship to the feet or the left heel, and sometimes even to the right or left toe. I have seen photographs with captions stating that the ball was opposite the right toe (which was in fact pointing at the ball because the toe was "turned in"), but in relationship to the line of flight the ball was actually opposite the left heel. This is an example of the acknowledged difficulty of positioning the ball correctly with an open stance. It is apparently even difficult to describe!

Really it is best not to think of the ball as being "so many inches" from a heel or toe, because these distances will—or should—vary with width of stance. To simplify the arithmetic in demonstrating this point, we will regard a golf ball as being one and a half inches in diameter. In the correct address position as described, the club head—not the ball—will be in line with the mid-point between the

D

heels. Therefore if the heels are only two inches apart, then half the ball will be opposite the left heel, the other half being "inside" the heel. With the heels four inches apart the front surface of the ball will be about half an inch inside the left heel. Heels eight inches apart places the front surface of the ball two and a half inches inside the left heel; while with the heels a foot apart the ball will be four and a half inches from the left heel.

That may seem a protracted description, but it is important, because with all the above different distances from the left heel, the ball is always just in front of a club head that is always midway between the heels.

It will be appreciated that with a shot with which we hope to hit a small target, accuracy of ball position might make all the difference between success and failure.

It will now be apparent that the only certain method of ensuring a correct ball position—especially when using an open stance—is to be sure that the club head position is correct; then, if the centre of it is not exactly and immediately behind the ball, to make it so, not by means of the hands, but by moving the feet, and therefore the whole "golfing machine"—i.e., yourself and the club.

THE ADDRESS FOR THE THREE SHOTS

First note the texture and grain of the grass, and whether it is dry, damp, or wet. The fastest green is a dry one, other things being equal. The ball will travel more quickly if the blades of grass "lean" away from the ball, than vice versa. Then note any gradients or curves between the ball and the hole. Now for preparation for the shot without undue fuss or delay.

Assume a good firm grip and approach the ball from behind; and try to discover the line on which you intend to send the ball, allowing for any curves of the green. At the same time, note a "spot" (by means of a bit of earth or different-coloured grass) on that line and about a foot or so in front of the ball. Don't lose sight of that spot, because it will look different when you are standing to the ball.

Now continue to approach the ball from behind, and apply the club head to the ball, with its face exactly at right angles to the line which runs from the ball to the "spot". Adjust your feet so that the right one is parallel to the club face, and only a few inches to the right of it; and draw the left foot back about five inches from the square stance, and place it about forty-five degrees to the right one.

Follow the line backwards from the club head to between your heels, and see that it is midway between them. If it is not, then your shoulders are probably not "square" enough, in which case turn them slightly to the right and move both feet slightly to the left.

Now glance at the "spot" to confirm that the club face is still at the correct angle. Finally squeeze the club shaft with both hands to make sure that you have a really firm grip; and push the hands down slightly to ensure maintenance of the arm–club angle; and glance at the target to see the distance and to estimate the strength of the shot—which you will do instinctively.

At that moment, when you look at the back of the ball and decide that you are going to "see it hit", you are ready to begin the back-swing.

The above description has taken much longer than should be taken on the performance. Remember that the strength is more important than the line, therefore visualise that two-foot trench, and get on with the shot, thinking only of the distance because you have put every part of yourself and the club in such a position that—providing you swing correctly—the line will be correct without any further thought or help from you.

THE SWING FOR THE THREE SHOTS

Theoretically, the only way the face of the putter can be kept entirely square to the hole, all the way on the back-swing and the forward swing, is to use an absolutely perpendicular shaft with the club head at right angles to it. Any advantage from that would be outweighed by the clumsy grip that would have to be used. Many of the methods of gripping, and also the different-angled putters, are designed to try to approach this ideal, but I am sure it is a mistake to try to do this by means of the hands, with the aid of unusual grips or swings.

If you gently swing an ordinary putter or other golf club to and fro—without any artificial anatomical aids—the club face is bound to open on the back-swing and close on the forward swing, even if only slightly. Now, if an attempt is made to prevent that natural opening on the back-swing, then the natural return from that on the forward swing would tend to be more shut than if you had not interfered.

Another disadvantage of this interference is that merely to try to hold the club face square on the back-swing is apt to make you look to see if it is square instead of watching the ball. There is the same possibility on the forward swing if you try to prevent the club face shutting—you will look to see if you are succeeding—and in addition you might even try so well that you actually open the face slightly about impact, thus pushing the ball to the right of the hole.

Not only will the aforementioned, and frequently advocated, interference produce the above possibilities— if not probabilities—but I will go further, and say that allowing the club face to open naturally on the back-swing will make it more likely to remain square at, and for a longer distance after, impact, so long as the swing is natural and no attempt is made to guide the club head.

So far we have really been discussing interference with the swing, and we should be satisfied that it is best avoided, by using a normal grip, exactly as with other clubs. As to the actual method of swinging the putter, there are three main possibilities to discuss, which may be combined in various degrees:

1. With the hand or hands, using the wrist or wrists as hinges.

2. With the arm or arms, using the shoulder or shoulders as hinges.

3. With the upper part of the body by revolving the shoulders, using the horizontal upper part of the spine as a hinge or hub.

What, then, are the advantages and disadvantages of the three methods of swinging?

1. Hands and Wrists. (*a*) Early wrist action on the back-swing is an all-too-common erroneous movement in all golf shots, and would therefore be better banished from the game as well as from the player's mind.

(*b*) All sorts of tricks are resorted to, to try to make the putt a one-hand-and-one-wrist shot, but since the other hand and wrist must also move, there is much room for error.

(*c*) The commonly recommended method—both with putts and chips—of deliberately cocking the wrists early in the back-swing, but also of preventing wrist action after impact, is an unnatural combination of movements, and is very liable to the human element of error, especially because it necessitates moving the hands forward at impact which had not been previously moved backwards—at any rate to the same extent.

(*d*) The entirely hand-and-wrist swing produces an arc that is not at all flattened, and is therefore too abruptly

up and down, and will probably have a dangerous amount
of club-face opening and shutting.

With so many disadvantages this method cannot have
any advantages.

2. Arms and Shoulder-joints. (*a*) This method, often
with bent arms, appears to be *thought* to be frequently
used. For example, several professionals claim in their
books to putt by the arms only without any body movement whatever. Their photographs belie their statements,
because they clearly show the left shoulder to be lower at
the end of the back-swing, and higher at the end of the
forward swing than at the address position. This is surely
proof that at least the upper part of the body has moved
by revolving around the upper part of the spine.

Furthermore, in photographs taken from "behind the
shot" of these same self-styled "arm putters", more of the
left knee can be seen at the end of the back-swing than at
address, while after impact the left knee cannot be seen at
all. That proves that the legs and therefore—of necessity—
the lower part of the body also moved.

(*b*) To putt by using the arms without moving the body
would necessitate a swing from the two hubs—i.e., the two
shoulder joints; and if the elbows were not bent at the
start, they would have to be during the course of the swing
—the right one on the back-swing, and the left one on the
forward swing.

If the reader will swing a putter from the shoulder-
joints, without letting his left "shoulder" change its position, he will realise the impossibility of the so-called
"arm swing without body movement".

(*c*) The frequently advocated accompaniment to this
swing, of trying to keep the club head near the ground on
both the back and forward swings, has several disadvantages. It tends to cause swaying, and divided attention
with the eyes, which try to watch the moving club head as

well as the ball. The club head is also apt to be kept low for too long, thus disturbing the rhythm of the swing, with a likelihood of anything but a square club face at impact.

The disadvantages of this method are too obvious to warrant further discussion; and in fact I think that those who believe they use it are deluding themselves.

3. Revolving the Shoulders around the Horizontal Upper Part of the Spine. Not only do I consider this to be the best method for the shots under consideration—which means they are played exactly as other golf shots, but in miniature—but I also believe that many of the experts use this method, some of them—as I have just proved, without knowing it!

In that belief I am in good company, for the great Bobby Jones, in his book "Down the Fairway", asserted that not only the body, but also the legs, do move when putting— even for short ones—"despite the popular notion to the contrary".

From my observations and study of photographs I have come to the conclusion that probably the majority of good putters use this method—often with needless embellishments—but in some cases there is a subtle difference in execution which deceives them, because some of the movements may be scarcely perceptible.

In a correctly executed golf stroke the movement begins around the upper part of the spine (the hub), and is transmitted via the arms (the spokes), to the club head (the rim). The other method—which is wrong—is to begin the movement by cocking the wrists with the hands, so that the body follows the club. That is what I believe the so-called hand, wrist, and arm putters do, because they are under the misapprehension that the left shoulder is too far away to control a shot such as a short putt. From experience I know that they are wrong. I believe this mistaken idea—which is very noticeable in the chip-shot—is due to the belief that a large amount of wrist-cocking is necessary on the back-swing. On the contrary, as with all golf shots, wrist-cocking should be completely involuntary and automatic, and just as much or as little is required as is developed by the momentum of the swing.

Regarding the natural use of muscles and joints, the normal return from *voluntary* wrist-cocking on the back-swing is a reverse wrist action immediately after impact, which all are agreed is undesirable.

Before going into the details of the method of executing this short swing, I will admit at the outset that when the reader first tries the method he will probably feel clumsy and awkward, and may be disinclined to persevere. I had that experience—so I know—but I was so convinced theoretically of its virtue that I gave it a good trial. I soon learned—maybe after four or five half-hourly sessions—to use the method, and now know its value.

Even the shortest putt, say of one foot, or the sort that you hope your opponent will concede, just in case you should miss it, can be easily and confidently sunk. I say "shortest putt" because this is the sort that is often missed owing to the mistaken belief that it is best "tapped" in with the hand. I have seen professionals miss two-foot putts, but I can vouch that the merest novice would not miss a two-foot putt by this method when he had become accustomed to it.

Now, as to the *modus operandi*. Having taken up the grip, stance, and address as described, with the hands fairly low on the shaft, and with the upper part of your back horizontal, let the arms hang straight down—in fact, push them gently down—so as to maintain the normal angle between the arms and the club shaft and to straighten the arms to the same extent as in any other golf shot. Make sure that you have a really firm grip with all parts of both hands, then you are ready to begin the back-swing simply by pushing the left shoulder down. The shoulder will go down only a tiny bit for a very short putt, and farther and farther down, according to the length of the shot.

Do not do anything voluntarily with your arms, wrists, hands, or the club. These movements will all happen automatically in their correct order. The arms will swing slightly from the shoulder-joints, carrying the hands and the club with them; also the wrists will cock—maybe imperceptibly—at the end of the back-swing. Don't get harassed if the wrists do not appear to cock—they will as much as necessary. That is the back-swing, which is performed slowly and unhurriedly, and now is the important moment.

You must feel that the back-swing is completed before beginning the forward swing. It may not be quite so—even though you feel that it is—because maybe the wrists are in process of cocking slightly, but that occurrence is involuntary, and therefore will not be unduly impressed on your consciousness. The rule is, "The shorter the shot the longer the wait". There must be that stop at the top to get rhythmic movement.

Then all you do is to reverse the motion by pulling your left shoulder upwards. The arms, hands, and the club will follow, and the slight opening of the club face which occurred on the back-swing will be undone, and the face will be square at impact and for an appreciable distance afterwards, before it begins to shut.

The swing is, of course, distinctly and very desirably upright. Also, the left shoulder going down, then up, gives a *feeling* of a sharp rise of the club head on the back-swing and the forward swing. Actually it ensures the reverse— i.e., a flat arc for a few inches—but without the dangers of keeping the club head low consciously.

In addition to the shoulder movement maintaining a flat arc for as long as necessary, the left shoulder going

upwards prevents the club head staying near the ground
for too long after impact, which is a very desirable feature
in both stymie play and putting.

A stymie played with the intention to follow through
close to the ground, as often advocated, is—I'm sure it will
be agreed—more dangerous and less successful, because it
might make you hit your opponent's ball if only six inches
away, or you might check the follow through owing to fear
of doing this. In fact, I am sure that that is the chief cause
of the apparent difficulty of stymie play. As the reader is no
doubt aware, checking the follow through often means
checking the blow, and consequent mis-hitting.

In putting, the advantage of the club head rising
reasonably soon after impact is that it ensures the ball
rolling from the start, in consequence of the top spin
imparted. This rolling from the start is generally considered to be the best method of propelling a golf ball on
the green. Further to this end, it is better to use a putter
with little or no loft.

I would warn the reader that if he relaxes the right-hand
grip before impact, the shot may have a "cracked-pot"
sound—especially with the putter—and go off line. It is
the firm right-hand grip that ensures the right arm coming
into the shot automatically at the right time, and also that
indescribable sweet sound that only "solid contact" can
produce.

If any difficulty is experienced with this, don't hesitate
to use deliberately the right arm, but even then the left
shoulder should still initiate the forward swing. Remember that these are slow shots, and that there is therefore
plenty of time to transfer your thoughts from one part of
your anatomy to another. Your thoughts should be trans-
ferred in accordance with the following formula: "left
shoulder down, stop; left shoulder up and right arm
through", the right arm being applied immediately the

left shoulder begins to go up. The fact that the left shoulder has lead the forward swing into the "groove" is sufficient to ensure it staying there.

Since there is plenty of time to think during the momentary stop at the top, some players may find it advantageous to pull the left shoulder up and to strike the ball with the right arm at the same time. This will usually give the feeling of hitting upwards, which is certain proof that the swing is correctly "in the groove". The reason you can use the right arm freely for these three shots is because the back-swing is rarely, if ever, beyond the "hitting area", where the right arm should come in. Even so, it is safer to feel that the left shoulder first begins to go upwards.

A final warning about the left-shoulder movement. It may be barely perceptible on short putts and stymies; in fact it may appear to be merely the means of setting the arms, or the club, moving in the correct direction; but it should always be the point of concentration, being, as it is, the nearest part to the horizontal upper part of the spine, which you wish to set in motion as the hub of the wheel.

All that I have said about putting applies also when using the centre-shafted putter. It remains now to say a few words in specific reference to the chip-shot and the stymie.

THE CHIP-SHOT

This little shot is usually played from just a little way off the green, and since I am suggesting playing it in the same manner as the putt, I consider that it is more easily played with a short-shafted club, not too remotely different in length from a putter.

Frequently, different clubs are recommended for different lengths of shot; but I prefer the method of mastering one club, knowing exactly what it will do, and using only that club for all chip-shots, increasing the length of the back-swing with the distance required.

The number seven is perhaps the most commonly used club for the purpose, and that is the one I prefer. The player should find from experience how far the ball will roll after landing from different distances, then he will know where to pitch the ball. Half an hour's practice should furnish that information. It will not, of course, roll as far as a ball played with a less lofted club, but I am sure that most people will be more accurate with the short-shafted number seven.

In playing the shot, get the line, as when putting, by means of a bit of soil or grass in front of the ball. Having assumed the address position as for a putt, decide the spot on the green where you wish the ball to land, then disregard the hole, and concentrate on the strength required to reach that spot—which is your target. The ball, having found your target, will roll the rest of the way into the hole, or very near it, requiring only one putt to hole out.

Regard the shot merely as a long putt played with a lofted club, and play it in all respects—both in preparation and execution—in exactly the same way. Do not make this a "different shot" by excessive use of the wrists, which is only a needless complication. "Left shoulder down, stop; left shoulder up and right arm through" is again the formula—and the necessary wrist work will occur automatically, if you grip firmly with all parts of both hands.

There is one exception to the use of the number seven for a ball which is a "chip-able" distance from the hole. That is when the hole is near "your edge" of the green, but with a bank or bunker intervening, necessitating the ball stopping very soon after crossing the obstacle. For that shot the number nine is the best club, played with the face opened; but it is really not a chip-shot, but a "cut-shot", and will be described in the next chapter.

THE STYMIE

Although the stymie has been abolished, the description of it is included for the benefit of those who may still wish to play it in private matches. In fact it might one day be officially thought preferable to the amount of "ball lifting" on the green now found to be necessary.

If your opponent's ball comes to rest on the green between your ball and the hole, and is six inches or more both from your ball and the hole, then you are stymied! What of it? The only people to whom supposedly difficult golf shots are difficult are those who do not take the trouble to learn how to play them. Played as described, the stymie can be learnt in half an hour.

All you have to learn is to disregard the ball in front, and then play a chip-shot. The shot can be played with any lofted club from the five to the nine, but I would strongly advise using only the chosen "chip-shot club"—i.e., the number seven. The elevation with this club will comfortably clear the front ball, so that detail need not be given a thought. Don't think of your problem as jumping the other ball, or that is all you will do—if you even do that. The club will take care of that.

Your problem is a simple one: you are going to play a chip-shot, and maybe only a tiny one, and you are going to play it as if it were a putt. You might use some portion of your opponent's ball as the "spot" for giving you the line. Having got that line, completely disregard the front ball and also the hole, thinking only of the strength required to chip the ball to the spot where you wish it to land.

The exact spot at which to aim is best discovered when practising the shot; and the only place to practise the shot is on a putting green. Don't be afraid of damaging the green, and don't be afraid of striking the other ball if it is only six inches away. You won't do either of these things if you remember to straighten your arms—especially the left one—at address, and swing as instructed. Again the formula is: "left shoulder down, stop; left shoulder up and right arm through"—gripping firmly with all parts of both hands, and leaving the wrists to function automatically.

CHAPTER IV

BALL SPIN: THE CUT-SHOT: INTENTIONAL SLICE AND HOOK

APPRECIATION of the principles of ball spin will add much to the enjoyment, understanding, and execution of the golf stroke.

As a golf ball travels through the air it is normally re-volving on its own axis. The direction in which it is spin-ning will depend on the direction of the blow which set it in motion. If the reader will visualise a golf ball with a long nail driven through its middle to represent its axis, he will realise that there are thousands of possible direc-tions in which the ball can spin, depending on the position in which the "axis" is held. But there are only four true spins—two vertical and two horizontal—in relationship to the forward propulsion of the ball; and also four oblique spins. It is the oblique spins which may be multiplied by any number.

See Diagram No. 6, in which the arrow on each "ball" indicates the direction in which it is spinning.

No. 1. Vertical top spin in which the ball revolves "forwards" in the same direction as it is travelling.

No. 2. Vertical bottom spin (or back spin), in which the ball revolves "backwards" in the opposite direction to its flight.

No. 3. Horizontal clockwise spin to the right.

No. 4. Horizontal anti-clockwise spin to the left.

No. 5. Oblique clockwise top spin to the right.

No. 6. Oblique anti-clockwise top spin to the left.

No. 7. Oblique clockwise back spin to the right.

No. 8. Oblique anti-clockwise back spin to the left.

It should be noted that the oblique spins are a combination of vertical and horizontal spins.

According to the direction in which the ball is spinning, it behaves differently while travelling through the air, and also on striking the ground. I will now describe this behaviour of the ball with different spins as numbered in the diagram, bearing in mind that numbers three and four are merely of theoretical interest, since a golf ball cannot be made to spin exactly horizontally with a golf club.

No. 1. As the top spin turns the ball over and over, it is working in conjunction with gravity, therefore the ball tends to come to earth, and then roll straight onwards.

No. 2. As the back spin turns the ball backwards, it is working against gravity, therefore the ball tends to climb, the trajectory being convex towards the earth. When the ball lands, the force of the forward motion may carry it a little onwards, but the back spin will check the motion, and may even cause the ball finally to roll a little backwards, just as a tennis ball, a billiard ball, or a hoop can be made to do.

No. 3. As the ball moves forward, spinning like a top, horizontally to the right on its vertical axis, it curves sharply to the right. On landing, any further forward movement is due to the blow; the spin causing the ball to curve further to the right.

No. 4. In all respects the same as No. 3, but curving to the left.

No. 5. In the air, this ball will curve to the right like No. 3, but not so sharply, owing to the combination of top spin and side spin; for the same reason it will come to earth sooner, and on landing will roll onwards to the right.

No. 6. In all respects the same as No. 5, but curving to the left.

No. 7.   Like No. 2, this ball will tend to soar owing to its back spin; and the clock-wise side spin will curve it to the right.   On landing, the ball will kick sharply to the right, the side spin tending to roll it to the right, while the back spin holds it back.

No. 8.   In all respects the same as No. 7, but curving and kicking to the left.

Little wonder that the inexperienced player without any knowledge of spin often finds it difficult to tame a golf ball! Study of the above details will teach the reader to know why an iron shot sometimes "unexpectedly" kicks to the right or left; also why a drive that appears to have been reasonably well hit can come soon to earth as though being pulled down; and also why a putt that has been "rolled" from the start with top spin will pleasingly go and on as though it had legs.   In addition, he will learn why a ball "slices", and subsequently be able to play a straight ball without difficulty.

It will no doubt be obvious that the faster the ball spins in any given direction, the greater will be the effect of the spin.   Therefore, other things being equal, the harder the ball is hit the more pronounced will be the curves due to spin.   Other facts worthy of note are that the smoother the club face—and especially if wet—the less it grips the ball, and therefore the less the spin; and, contrariwise, the rougher the club face—and especially if dry—the more it grips the ball, and therefore the more the spin.

Theoretically, disregarding for the moment which type of club is being used, to produce top spin the ball should be struck above its horizontal equator—i.e., on its upper half; but actually, top spin is also applied if the club face contacts the ball a little below its middle if the club head is moving upwards as well as forwards.   That is what often happens to a drive, and for that reason I think it best to tee the ball high. (Bobby Jones always tee-d the ball one inch from the ground for a drive.) By this means you tend to deliver a "flat" blow well below the horizontal equator, with little if any top spin to pull the ball to earth.

Regarding the irons, especially the higher numbers—and even the lofted woods—when playing the ball off the ground without a tee, I doubt if it is possible to have struck the ball other than with back spin if it becomes properly airborne. If the reader will apply the face of his clubs in turn to a golf ball on a table, and carefully note the point of contact, he will see what I mean. Of course a topped ball will have top spin, but it will not rise properly into the air. Just as top spin can be applied even if the club head contacts the ball a little below its equator, so also can back spin be applied even though the club head contacts the ball a little above the equator, providing that the club head is still travelling downwards—i.e., has not yet reached the bottom of its arc.

Briefly, then, No. 1 is the ideal spin for a putt or when it is desired to make the ball roll. No. 2 is the inevitable normal golf spin with any straightforward shot, probably with all clubs except the driver and the putter, and certainly with all irons. Nos. 3, 5, and 7, or any combination of them will produce various degrees of slice; while Nos. 4, 6, and 8, or any combination of them, will produce various degrees of hook.

THE CUT-SHOT

Briefly, this shot is a slice played with a lofted club, but with the idea of making the ball rise quickly and steeply, and stop almost immediately on landing. The ball does not normally curve to the right while in the air, but on landing may curve a few inches to a foot or so to the right.

Since the method of playing the shot is to lay open the face of the club so as to give it more lofting power than it normally possesses, then obviously the club to use is the number nine. It is wise not to overdo the face opening, as you might then have the face practically horizontal, and be in danger of striking the ball with its edge—i.e., of topping it—with disastrous consequences. Another danger is that the toe of the club would point so far backwards—thus narrowing the available striking edge of the club to such an extent—that the ball might be missed altogether.

This shot should not be made a habit with all niblick work, which would be on a par with the thoughtless tennis-player who uses the back spin forehand drive *ad nauseam*. It should be reserved for those occasions when it is the best shot to play—i.e., when the ball has to be played from near the green over an obstacle such as a bank or bunker—or maybe from a bunker flanking the green in certain circumstances—and especially if the hole is near "your side" of the green, so that you wish the ball to stop almost dead on landing. Another instance when this shot might be the one to use, is when the ball is a little way off the green, but too near to a fence or hedge to allow room for the back-swing of a normal shot.

To play the cut-shot you are usually told to open the club face and to use a very open stance. I think that is the wrong attitude to the shot, as you will then usually have the ball too far back, and the "shoulder stance" not open enough. A much safer method is to think of the stance as square, but aiming well to the left. If the reader will map out these two methods on the floor, he will find the all-important ball position to be entirely different.

The method which I am advising will put the club head in a position midway between the heels in relationship to the square stance, aiming to the left. The degree of aiming to the left is determined by the degree of club face opening, which also determines the direction of the ball's flight, as the reader will learn in a moment.

A very important point is the method of taking up the address position. See Diagram No. 7. Rest the club head on the ground, with the face opened to the extent considered necessary, remembering that the further it is open the more vertically the ball will rise. Assume the normal grip—and grip really firmly with both hands—and then approach the ball from behind, and while you are almost facing the target, apply the heel end of the club face to the ball, so that the face is at right angles to the intended flight of the ball—i.e., to the line to the target.

Now comes the critical adjustment of the feet. Disregard the peculiar appearance of the club head, and think of the bottom end, or neck, of the shaft as the club head, which should be in line with the mid-point between your heels, the club shaft being at right angles to the intended line of the swing. That is a very important point—in fact the crux of the whole matter—because if you think of the shot, as often described, as being played with an open stance, then you tend to get the club shaft at right angles to the target line, in which case the ball will be too far back.

The swing is just the normal straightforward one from a square stance, as though you were going to send the ball thirty to forty degrees to the left of the target. At impact, the heel end of the club face makes contact with the ball, which receives a glancing blow from heel to toe of the club face, thus sending the ball towards the target with clockwise oblique back spin.

Whether you use a half, three-quarter, or full swing will depend on the height the ball is intended to go. The individual player can best determine this fact by a few moments' practice, but generally speaking the ball must always be struck decisively.

Perhaps the most important point regarding the swing is that when ready to begin it by pushing the left shoulder down, having decided upon the "strength" required, the target should be entirely disregarded, and a normal "square stance shot" played.

INTENTIONAL SLICE AND HOOK

Most professionals appear to be of the opinion that players should not attempt these shots early in their golfing career, if at all. I most heartily disagree with them. I "had a slice" for years simply because I did not thoroughly understand how it was produced. I had of course heard in a a vague sort of way that a slice could be caused by an open club face, an open stance, or an outside-to-in swing; but that knowledge did not teach me how to avoid these faults. I have since learned that in golf, as in all other things in life, the best way to avoid doing things the wrong way is to know and understand the wrong way. In life generally, it is called profiting by your mistakes, and, as has been truly said, the man who never made a mistake never made anything! As applied to golf, if a player learns how to slice and hook at will, and therefore to know exactly how he does it, then he knows what to avoid when requiring a straight shot, and the shot will be straight.

In my opinion, based on experience, an embryo golfer should learn the principles of ball spin, and how to slice and hook, as soon as he is able to get the ball into the air.

With regard to the different types of spin already discussed, to add to our store of knowledge it will be worth while remembering the following rule. Whether playing a slice or a hook, as the number of the irons becomes higher, there is less effect on the ball as it travels through the air, but more after landing. For example, a ball sliced with a number one iron will curve to the right in the air and follow approximately the same line on landing; but the same shot played with a number nine will usually make the ball travel straight while in the air, but curve more sharply to the right on landing.

The Slice. It will now be apparent that to play a slice, the face of the club must strike the ball a glancing blow in the direction from outside the target line to inside the target line. This can be done by either of two ways, or by a combination of both.

1. Open the face of the club, then take the normal grip, and use the normal square stance. The ball is addressed by the heel end of the club face, and although the club head swings straight through the ball, the ball is first contacted to the left of its vertical centre, and will therefore tend to "slip along the club face" towards the toe, thus developing clockwise spin and a consequent slice owing to the glancing blow. Note that this slice is caused by the club face contacting that surface of the ball which faces the player, even though the club head is travelling towards the target.

1 (a). A variation of the above method is to address the ball with a square club face, but having first turned both hands—that is, the entire grip—to the left. This abnormal position of the hands is said to change to the normal position during the course of the swing, thus having the club face open at impact. It is well to understand that this wrong hand position may produce a slice, but I do not like the method for intentionally slicing, because the faulty hand position at address alters the whole set-up of the body, including the left shoulder being too low and the right arm too far forward. A faulty address causes a "faulty" feel, and therefore favours a faulty swing—and uncertainty.

2. Open the stance, but keep the face of the club square. In this case the slice is produced by the swing, which carries the club head across the ball, heel to toe, from outside-to-in, even though the club face is square to the target at

impact, and strikes the back of the ball. There are two objections to this method. First the acknowledged difficulty of correctly positioning the ball with an open stance, these possible different ball positions producing different and uncertain results; and secondly, the ability to hit a straight shot from an open stance is likely to assert itself, particularly when you wish it otherwise.

3. An open club face—or the grip turned to the left—plus an open stance, should theoretically produce the effects of both, more definitely than either alone, but there are still the objections to the open stance and the faulty grip.

In my experience, the simplest and most accurate way to slice intentionally is to depend entirely on the open club face, using an ordinary square stance and ball position, normal grip and normal swing. Then everything feels exactly the same as with a normal swing.

The direction and degree of the slice can be varied in two ways.

1. The more the club face is opened, the higher the ball will rise and the sooner it will turn right. Conversely, the ball can be made to travel farther in a straight line, and with a lower trajectory before turning to the right, by opening the club face less. It should be noted that if the driver is used, and the face much opened, then the ball should be tee-d high, because the back of the club head resting on the ground will raise the club face into a higher position.

2. By turning the square stance more and more to the left—i.e., aiming to the left—the ball can be made to turn to the right around an obstruction farther and farther away.

These two methods of varying the degree of slice can, of course, be used together. For example, a normal square stance and a very open face would turn the ball quickly to the right, whereas a square stance aimed to the left and a slightly open face would delay the ball's turning to the right, as well as reduce the amount of slice.

See Diagram No. 8 in which there are three square stances and three ball trajectories similarly numbered. In each case the ball starts its journey in line with the stance. The trajectories indicated curving round the three trees at progressively increasing distances are of course diagrammatic and not necessarily accurate, but they serve to demonstrate the principle.

In a nutshell, then, to play intentionally an average slice, take up a normal square stance, the whole body— i.e., the aim—being turned somewhat to the left. The ball must be in the normal position in relation to the stance assumed (not farther back in the open stance position), and addressed by the heel end of the club face, with the face open. A normal grip should be taken after opening the club face. Execute a normal "square stance swing" by pushing the left shoulder down then pulling it up.

The Hook. I am quite certain that this is the most difficult shot in the whole game of golf. However, I still believe that the novice should attempt it, and at least understand its theory, because being concerned with spin, and being in all respects the exact opposite to the slice, it will improve the understanding of these subjects.

It is as difficult to hook as it is easy to slice, but the methods advocated to produce a hook will serve to demonstrate the dangers of these grips, stances, and swings, when attempting to play a straight shot. The difficulty of the shot is made apparent by the divergent methods recommended by the experts.

Many professionals advocate merely turning the hands well to the right on the club shaft, and addressing the ball with a square club face which is supposed to shut during the course of the swing.

My objection to this method is the same as it is to playing a slice this way; the unusual hand position at address alters the set-up of the body, including making the left shoulder too high and the right arm too near the body, and therefore of necessity making the swing feel different, with consequent uncertainty as to results.

Other methods recommended include various combinations of the following adjustments: a closed stance, the ball nearer the right foot, a flat back-swing, and a conscious wrist-roll at impact.

These are all much too complicated and uncertain in result. Also, flat swings and voluntary wrist-roll are best left out of a golfer's make-up.

Theoretically, a hook can be played by the same methods as a slice, but "in reverse"—i.e., by the use of a shut club face, or a closed stance, or both together; the effect being, similarly to strike the ball a glancing blow, the difference being that the toe end of the club face is the first part to contact the ball as the club head travels from inside to outside the target line. I say "theoretically", because it is as difficult to hook as it is easy to slice!

Briefly, then, the simplest and most reliable way to attempt to play a hook is to shut the club face, then take a normal grip, then assume a normal square stance, the whole body being turned somewhat to the right so that you are aiming to the right, the ball being in the correct position relative to the assumed square stance (and not further forward as for a closed stance), and being addressed by the toe end of the face of the club. Execute a normal square stance swing by pushing the left shoulder down, then pulling it up.

Diagram No. 8—depicting the variations of the slice—can also be applied to the hook, by visualising the trajectories curving in the opposite direction around the other side of the trees; and the stances aiming to the right instead

of to the left. Also, the same rules apply "in reverse"—
i.e., the more the club face is shut, the less the ball will rise
and the sooner it will turn left; and the less the face is
shut, the later in the ball's flight, and the less will it turn
left. This late or very slight turning to the left is sometimes referred to as a "draw".

Finally, I will once again stress that to produce the
necessary spin to cause a slice, and more so for a hook, the
ball must be struck decisively, and the grip must be firm.

CHAPTER V

SUNDRY DIFFICULTIES

THESE problems will be considered under the sub-titles of "Bunker Shots", "Awkward Lies", "Shots from the Rough", and "The Weather".

The average golfer never ventures beyond the fringe of these subjects, thereby missing at least half the pleasure of playing golf. He is always a little uncertain what to do in any such circumstance, and glad when it is over. Knowing the "difficult", renders the "straightforward" much easier; and when the reader is thoroughly conversant with what follows, he will be able to play an infinite variety of shots with confidence, then he will begin to enjoy "the spice of life".

(A) BUNKER SHOTS

The intelligent study of bunker shots is chiefly a study of angles, both of the implements and of the terrain.

The approximate loft of all clubs is shown in Diagram No. 1. Some books describe the loft of a club as the angle which the "back" of the face makes with the horizontal, according to which, the loft of the number three iron would be sixty-five degrees; but I prefer the other method, which regards the loft as the angle formed by the front of the club face and the perpendicular (or the club shaft), which makes the loft of a number three twenty-five degrees. This latter is a useful measurement, as it conveys what you can actually see, and also because the line at which the ball leaves the club face forms with the ground the same twenty-five degree angle, and therefore has some bearing on the shot. (See Diagrams Nos. 9 and 10.) This is a very important fact to understand, because the sameness of these angles applies to all clubs, providing the ball is not tee-d up, and is correctly struck so that it leaves the club face at right angles to it.

The two diagrams on bunker shots should be carefully studied in conjunction with what follows.

Many players make the mistake of taking out their niblicks or "blasters" immediately they know their ball is in a bunker. I think this idiocy is encouraged by that stupid remark "Well out, partner", which is often made when someone sends his (or her) ball high into the air with a niblick, when he could have sent it, say, 150 yards nearer the hole—or maybe on to the green—with a number three iron. There is nothing clever in "getting out" of a bunker—and nothing difficult if a little thought is given to the matter. You are not "well out" if you play from a bunker flanking the green into another on the other side.

In these circumstances, if I am with people whom I know well enough to say "Rotten shot", some of them think I am being facetious. But I'm not! I cannot understand players being satisfied with such a low standard of play. In golf—as in all things in life, for that matter—we should always "aim high". As has been said—by whom I don't know—"Aim at the moon and you may hit the wall; aim at the wall and you'll stay in the ditch". A bunker shot is not "good" unless you get all the distance which the height of the bunker wall and the "lie" will allow, when distance is required—or from a bunker flanking the green, unless you can hole out in one putt. The latter is a better shot still if the ball is on the line to the hole; and even better again if in the hole. Don't think of "holing out from a bunker" as necessarily a fluke; the shot is always "on" if you gauge correctly the "line" and the "strength". The foregoing diatribe is not wasted if it stimulates ambition!

Choice of Club. What, then, should you do on finding your ball in a bunker? The first consideration should be the "lie", by which I am particularly referring to the depth of the ball in the sand. If the ball is well into the sand, you will need a niblick or a modern sand wedge. If the ball is "sitting up", or nearly so, then the choice of club depends on the position of the bunker. If the bunker is near the green you choose the club which will clear the bunker wall and put the ball near the hole. That club will most often be the number nine. If the bunker is "away back", you choose the club which will give you the distance you require, providing that it will also make the ball clear the wall of the bunker. If the club of your choice for distance will not "clear the wall", then you use the one that will just do that.

In making your decision on choice of club, you will need to determine the following facts.

1. The depth of the bunker wall, measured from the top down to the level at which you will stand—i.e., to the (what may be imaginary) intersection of wall and floor. See Diagrams Nos. 9 and 10.

2. The distance the ball is from the same "bottom corner" of the wall.

3. The angle the ball's flight will have to make with the floor to clear the bunker wall.

4. The loft of the club you will require to use. This club will have the same loft as the angle required to clear the wall.

Reference to Diagram No. 9 will show that if the wall is one foot deep (preferably a shade less), and the ball one foot from the intersection of wall and floor, then you will need forty-five degrees elevation to clear the wall, therefore you should use the number seven, which has forty-five degrees of loft.

If the ball is two feet from the wall, you will need only

thirty-five degrees elevation, which you can get with the thirty-five degree lofted number five and gain at least twenty yards.

If the ball is three feet from the wall, you will need only twenty-five degrees elevation, which you can get with the twenty-five degree lofted number three, and gain forty yards on the number seven.

To quote further examples applied to Diagram No. 9, but with the wall two feet high instead of one foot. You would need number five in place of number three and number seven in place of number five. The number nine, having only fifty degrees of loft, used in place of number seven, would not clear the wall unless you opened the face enough to make its loft—and therefore the ball elevation— equal to sixty-eight degrees.

To the uninitiated all this may seem very complex and difficult, but actually, once the principle is understood, it is very simple and can be "taken in at a glance". I will put it more simply. The important landmark is the intersection of the bunker wall and floor. If this is the same distance (however great or small) from the top of the wall and the ball, then you obviously require just over forty-five degrees elevation (call it forty-five for simplicity's sake), and therefore you would use the number seven, which has forty-five degrees of loft. But if the ball is twice as far from the "intersection" as is the top of the wall, then thirty-five degrees elevation will clear the wall, therefore the number five (with thirty-five degrees loft) will do. The third example is: if the distance of the ball from the intersection of floor and wall is only half that to the top of the wall, then you will require sixty-eight degrees of elevation to clear the wall; therefore the only possible club to use is the number nine, with the face opened sufficiently to give an additional eighteen degrees loft above the niblick's normal fifty degrees.

It should be noted that if the bunker floor is sloping, due allowance should be made, because an "uphill lie" will require less elevation, while a "downhill lie" will require more. This calculation will be described under "Awkward Lies".

Briefly then, all you have to do is to note the relative distance of ball and top of wall from the intersection of wall and floor, then, with the foregoing data in mind, the elevation required, and therefore the club to use, may be determined at a glance.

Remember that the number three has twenty-five degrees loft and therefore produces twenty-five degrees elevation; then add five degrees loft and elevation for each successive club—leaving number eight out of the reckoning—number seven having forty-five, and number nine fifty, degrees.

A word about "taking a risk" to save the game or the hole: if the estimated measurements indicate that a number nine with fifty degrees loft is necessary, it is not only futile, but foolish, to try for more distance with, say, a number five, with only thirty-five degrees loft. Such a ball would be bound to hit the bunker wall, even if struck by the best player in the world.

An interesting fact is depicted in the other bunker diagram (No. 10)—viz., since the loft of any club is the same angle as the elevation of the ball which it will produce, therefore if the striking edge of any club is held just above the ball, while the shaft is parallel to the bunker floor, then the club face will be in line with the flight of the ball if struck with *that* club. This fact, if thought necessary, can most readily be used as an aid to practice at finding the angle of flight, by holding the club near its neck with the shaft parallel to the floor of the bunker; then, with the toe of the club head towards your face, you can see at a glance the line of the club face, which, continued, will form a line parallel to the line of flight of the ball if struck with that club.

All the aforementioned estimations require only a fraction of the time necessary to describe them, and of course are done outside the bunker, during the few seconds when you are noticing the lie.

"Choice of club", then, naturally follows consideration of the lie, and I make no apology for spending so much time on it, because the use of the proper implement, or tool, is at least half the battle in doing any job of work.

The Five Rules. There are five rules which apply to all bunker shots.

1. Decide on the club you are going to use and—if possible—the type of shot you are going to play, before entering the bunker.

2. Take up a very firm and accurate grip before entering the bunker.

3. As you step into the bunker note the consistency, condition, and depth of the sand, if any!

4. In assuming the stance, wriggle your feet to get a good firm footing.

5. In addressing the ball, the club head must not be grounded. This is the real difficulty of any bunker shot, because you must allow for the fact that the club head must be lower at impact than at address.

I have never read any suggestions as to how this should be done, but would advise seeing which of the following two methods produces the better result. Address the "ball" just above the sand, cock the left wrist a fraction— which will raise the clubhead a little—and place its heel behind the "ball"; then straighten the left arm as with any shot, to cause the club head to descend nearer the sand; or address the ball normally with the club head near the sand, but don't stretch the left arm.

Choice of Shot. Now that we know the "rules", how to assess the lie, and to choose the club, we must decide on the type of shot to use. We have the choice of four shots, and it is necessary to understand how they work and what they will do.

1. The explosion shot, in which a "divot" of sand—of variable length and depth—is taken behind the ball, the ball being "exploded" into the air by a cushion of sand. The club head does not contact the ball at all.

2. The clean shot, in which the club face makes direct contact with the ball, just as with a fairway shot.

3. The semi-explosion shot is a "cross" between the previous two, inasmuch as the club face does contact the ball, but only after taking a small sand "divot". That is, it is not quite "clean".

4. The cut-shot, which is the same in all respects as the cut-shot already described, but it may be either the "explosion", or the "clean", or the "semi-explosion" variety.

One or other of these methods may be the best way to play a particular shot, depending on several factors, including the location of the bunker. To avoid repetition in this description, I will refer to a bunker near the green as a "green bunker", and to one farther back as a "fairway bunker".

It can be accepted as a general rule that if there is good depth of sand in a bunker—even if it is moderately wet, but more especially if it is dry—the ball will almost invariably be partly submerged by the sand; in which case the best shot—and maybe the only one—will be an explosion shot, whether from a green bunker or a fairway bunker. On the other hand, if—as often happens—there is very little sand in the bunker, then the clean shot—or maybe the semi-explosion shot—will perhaps usually be

E

better, especially when distance is required as from a
fairway bunker.

I will now describe more specifically the indications for
a particular type of shot, of which there are four from a
green bunker and four from a fairway bunker.

1. *Green Bunker.* The explosion shot is the most frequently required, particularly if the ball is partly submerged
by the sand. It is used for the purpose of making the
ball rise quickly and stop quickly on landing, which is
especially necessary if the distance to be traversed is very
short.

2. *Green Bunker.*   The clean shot is just like an ordinary
fairway shot, and may be used when the ball is "sitting up",
preferably as a chip-shot from a shallow bunker, but also
when more distance is required than could be got with an
explosion shot.

3. *Green Bunker.* The semi-explosion shot is useful
when the ball is slightly under the sand so that it cannot be
taken "clean", or when there is not enough sand under
the ball for an explosion shot.

4. *Green Bunker.* The cut-shot—although advocated
by some professionals—is best avoided if possible,
especially if "taking sand", because the laying back—or
opening—of the club face reduces the available amount of
the striking edge. The shot might be indicated in certain
circumstances; for example, the ball might be so near the
back ledge of the bunker as to preclude a normal back-
swing, or you might require additional loft if the front wall
of the bunker is very high.

5. *Fairway Bunker.* The explosion shot will be necessary if the ball is well into the sand, or maybe if additional
elevation is required.

6. *Fairway Bunker.* The clean shot should be played
whenever possible because it will give the greatest distance,

but the ball must be "sitting up". It is the only shot to attempt with a wooden club.

7. *Fairway Bunker*. The semi-explosion shot is applicable when the ball is not quite sitting up. Don't attempt this shot with a "wood", but it can be played with any iron club, just as you would a ball in a "cuppy lie" on the fairway (described under "shots from the rough"), with the hands slightly ahead of the club head, and remembering to allow for the consequent slight loss of loft, and ball elevation. This shot gives distance somewhere between an explosion shot and a clean shot—more often nearer the latter—depending on the amount of sand taken before the ball.

8. *Fairway Bunker*. The cut-shot. Indications and objections are the same as in the case of a green bunker.

The Stance and Ball Position. The stance and ball position are important in bunker play. If the shot is to be played as a "cut-shot" or a "chip-shot", then use the stance already described for those shots from the fairway—but that will probably not be often.

For an ordinary explosion, semi-explosion, or a clean shot always use a wide square stance and so avoid any tendency to cut across the ball, which would reduce the available striking surface of the club head. There is the additional advantage that the stance is then in no way different from that used for fairway shots. Why complicate matters by using a different stance?

This cutting across the ball from outside-to-in—which is more likely with an open stance—is especially dangerous with an explosion shot, since the club head contacts the sand, one, two, or even three inches behind the ball. Since the ball is usually therefore well to the left, it might be missed altogether, or only the toe of the club head go under it, with insufficient forward propulsion to "lift" it out of the bunker. When taking up the stance for an explosion shot do not address the ball at all, in fact don't look at it. Address and look at the spot on the sand which you propose to hit; and that spot should be in the position in relationship to your feet where the ball would be for a fairway shot.

With the clean shot the ball position is the same as for a similar shot from the fairway—i.e., not so far to the left—therefore there is less danger from an "outside-to-in open stance swing", but the square stance is still the better as for all shots, as it ensures the club head—and the ball—travelling towards the target.

For a semi-explosion shot, the ball will be about midway between the heels or even farther to the right—the hands being somewhat ahead of the ball. Here again, the forward moving club head from a square stance will give more certain contact with the ball, and a greater distance.

The Swing. When playing bunker shots there is not much to be said about the swing, but what there is, is important, especially with the explosion shot.

An explosion shot should almost invariably be a full shot, hit with full force, no matter how short the distance the ball is required to travel. The distance the ball travels is regulated by the distance behind the ball that the club head contacts the sand. The nearer to the ball this occurs the farther the ball will go. Contrariwise, the farther from the ball the club head contacts the sand the less distance will the ball travel, owing to the bigger cushion of sand between the club head and the ball.

Another important point to note is that the farther the ball is to the left of where the club head contacts the sand, the more nearly vertically will it rise. I have not read any adequate explanation of this, but it seems reasonable to surmise that the farther past "impact" (with the sand) the club head "influences" the ball, the more loft it will have, and therefore the more approaching the vertical will the ball rise—and with less "life" since the club head is moving forwards. I am sure that this is the correct explanation in those cases where the player's left wrist "hinges" forward after impact.

This "vertical rising" of a ball played well to the left can be utilised, in preference to the cut-shot, when a little additional elevation is required, or when it is desired that the ball should stop beside the hole which is just over the bunker wall.

The explosion shot should be practised from a fairway bunker, to give the player confidence to hit really hard, and to learn what a short distance the ball goes. Knowing that—from experience—is very important, because many players make the mistake of not hitting hard enough, or of changing their minds—through fear and ignorance—after they had decided to hit hard.

At the same time it is no use hitting hard three inches behind the ball if there is only half an inch of sand in the bunker, because the club head could not get deeply enough under the ball. In that case the sand should be contacted maybe one inch behind the ball, and the shot played less forcibly. How rarely one sees anybody practising bunker shots! And yet, all that I have said about them could be learnt with a few hours experimenting with different clubs, different ball positions, and different depths and conditions of sand.

There is nothing to be said about the method of swinging for bunker shots, except that it is exactly as for other shots; i.e., left shoulder down, stop, left shoulder up more quickly. This—on the forward swing—will cause the club head to go down, then forward, then up into a full "follow through"; instead of burying itself in the sand as is often seen.

(B) AWKWARD LIES

There are four main varieties of uneven lies, viz.—left or right foot higher than the other, and both feet higher or lower than the ball. Any rules regarding these lies apply equally whether they are on the fairway, in the rough, or in a bunker.

Considering that probably about half the shots—excluding putts—played during any round of golf are from uneven lies, not enough space is devoted to this subject in most golf books. In addition, the descriptions that are available are too varied, and without sufficient explanation to give the learner confidence, or for him to understand why opinions differ.

Downhill and Uphill Lies. When the lie is downhill or uphill, the player has one foot at a lower level than the other.

It is usually recommended to play the ball nearer one foot than the other, and to use a stronger or weaker club than for the same shot on level ground—reasons given for these adjustments not always being the same. Other recommendations are concerned with the manner of "standing to" the ball, which of course includes the stance. I consider this the most important single item in these shots, since the swing and the balance are thereby affected.

Some professionals advocate keeping the body at right angles to the slope of the ground, which necessitates having more weight on the lower leg; whilst others advise keeping the body actually perpendicular, by bending the knee of the leg which is on higher ground. With both these methods of standing, some use a square stance, and others use an open stance. That means that the experts among them use four different methods of doing only one part of each of these shots.

It appears doubtful whether one particular method

would suit all ordinary mortals, but I am driven to the conclusion—after frequent experiment—that there is one best method. I am convinced that the simplest, and most easily mastered and remembered way is to use a square stance with the body perpendicular to—that is, at right angles to—the slope; because then, the stance, the shape of the body, and the swing, are in no way different from any ordinary shot, for which reasons the results are more consistent.

Effects of Stance. Having decided how to stand to the ball, we must fully appreciate how that affects the weight distribution, the shape of the body, the balance, and the angle of the club shaft and consequently the position of the club head.

Of necessity there will be more weight on the lower leg— i.e., on the left leg on a downhill lie, and on the right leg on an uphill lie—because the body will be "tilted" in that direction to maintain balance.

With a reasonably wide stance the lower leg carrying the weight will be actually about perpendicular; but the balance —which is all important—will be improved if the stance is made a little wider so that this weight-bearing lower leg slants somewhat outwards towards the foot.

It should be particularly noted that with the body in this correct "leaning position", the club shaft should be "in line" with the body. (That is, in the same relationship to the body as when addressing a ball on level ground). In other words, with an uphill lie the club head should be "ahead" of your hands; while with a downhill lie it should be "behind" your hands.

At this stage I would advise the reader to put himself, gripping a club, into the positions described, so as to sense the feeling of "pointing the club" forwards or backwards.

Above is the correct description of what is usually

described as putting more weight on one leg, and having the ball nearer the left foot on an uphill lie, and nearer the right foot on a downhill lie.

Throughout the swing the aim should be to keep the weight where it is in the beginning, which will be assisted by the wide stance and the "slanting" lower weight-bearing leg. If necessary further assistance can be had by gripping the ground with the toes. There will of course be some slight weight transference but it will be reduced to a minimum, probably with a curtailed follow through, which is all to the good in this type of shot in maintaining balance—especially with a downhill lie—thus ensuring a straight shot.

Choice of Club. Regarding the choice of club for the shot, you are usually told to use a club which will send the ball higher on a downhill lie, and lower on an uphill lie. It is desirable—and easy—to be more accurate than that. Estimate the angle of the slope to level ground, and suppose you believe it to be twenty degrees, and are playing downhill. With the club you would normally use for that shot on level ground, you will obviously lose twenty degrees elevation. For example, if you use a number five with thirty-five degrees loft and elevation, the ball will rise, not thirty-five degrees, but thirty-five less twenty, which is fifteen degrees—above the line of level ground. Therefore, on a twenty degree downhill slope, to get about the same elevation of the ball as you would on level ground with a number five, you will need to use a number nine. Stated otherwise, the twenty degrees which you lose on the slope, you have to gain on the club face. See Diagram No. 11.

In playing uphill lies, the same principle applies, but "in reverse"; i.e., the twenty degrees gained on the uphill slope must be subtracted from the loft of the club which you would use for the shot on level ground. Therefore instead of the number five you would use a number one. See Diagram No. 12. It will be apparent that this shot on a twenty degree uphill lie, played with a number five with thirty-five degrees loft, would give the ball a trajectory—relative to level ground—exceeding even that of a number nine, with the loss of thirty to forty yards in length.

The principle I have just enunciated, of adding to the club exactly what is lost on the slope—and vice versa—is very simple; but unfortunately it may not work out exactly as stated because the human body—and for that matter any other body, of reasonable size, that walks the earth—subconsciously tries to keep itself perpendicular.

For example, anyone walking along the side of a hill with one foot higher than the other, does so with the higher leg bent. Again, when jumping a fence on horseback, the rider's body would be tilted backwards if he did not lean forward as the horse rises; and as the horse goes downwards on taking the fence the rider leans backwards—if he wants to stay in the saddle; unless he is experienced enough in the more difficult "English Method" of leaning forward to reduce the weight on the horse's hind legs on landing. It is all a matter of trying to maintain balance by remaining perpendicular and thus preserving our centre of gravity.

Now if you apply this knowledge to an uphill lie at golf, even though you decide to put all your weight on the lower right leg and to hold your body at right angles to the slope, there will still be a tendency subconsciously to stand vertically by bending the left leg. Similarly, if the other method is used—i.e., bending the leg which is on higher ground—there is a subconscious tendency to put more weight on the lower leg simply because that is the side of the body needing most support.

The truth is that standing actually vertically with the higher leg bent, is the better way to maintain balance, but

—and we are playing golf—standing perpendicularly to the slope with more weight on the lower leg, will permit a better golf swing, much nearer the normal, with no danger of striking the ground before the ball on a downhill lie.

The net result is that instead of a twenty degree slope adding twenty degrees to the loft of the club, it usually adds only about ten degrees—i.e., half the expected amount.

From the foregoing facts, it would appear likely that the aforementioned different methods recommended by different professionals, do not differ so much as their respective advocates may think.

We are now in a position to formulate a reasonably accurate working rule:—For each ten degrees of uphill slope subtract five degrees from the loft of the club by using the next less-lofted one; and for each ten degrees of downhill slope add five degrees to the loft of the club by using the next more lofted one.

Finally, to put the whole matter in a nutshell:—with uphill or downhill lies use respectively one club stronger or weaker for each ten degrees of slope, use a wide stance, try to keep most weight on the lower leg, have the club shaft in line with your body, that is—like your body—at right angles to the slope, and swing normally by pushing the left shoulder down, and then pulling it up.

Now a word of warning! It may not be generally realised that to our eyes—five or six feet above the ground—slopes usually appear to be greater than they are. It is quite instructive—as I have frequently done—to estimate the angle of a slope to the horizontal, and then to measure it and find it to be little more than half what you thought. The angle is easily measured with the aid of two golf clubs as follows. Lay a golf club on the ground in the line of the slope, then raise the lower end until the shaft is horizontal. Then, hold the second club vertically at right angles to the first one—both touching the ground at the same spot.

Now see how many times the angle of the slope—which is under the horizontal club shaft—fits into the right angle above it. If it is three times, the angle is thirty degrees; if six times, then the angle is fifteen degrees. By doing this a few times the player will learn to judge slopes more accurately.

High and Low Lies. Regarding uneven lies with both feet higher or with both feet lower than the ball, the first thing to remember is that they both require the same number of adjustments, and that the adjustments for one are the exact opposite to those for the other. Once the reader has a clear conception of this, these supposedly difficult shots will become practically no more difficult than any other. Time spent studying them will be well repaid. See comparative table and Diagram No. 13.

These two varieties of shot will be better understood if considered together. Instead of merely stating that these "lies" tend to cause a slice or a hook, I will show why the ball goes off line, and how to accurately offset this occurrence.

Visualise a ground slope as vertical as a wall, then it will be clear that with the ball so high above the feet (level with your face) that the horizontal swing of the club would be bound to "pull" the ball round the left side of the player. Careful thought will show that this is neither a hook nor a pull, but that it is the trajectory of the ball's flight lying on its side. Before proceeding, will the reader grip a club and demonstrate that fact to his own satisfaction.

Leaving out of account the effects of gravity (because the fact is not thereby appreciably altered), if it were possible to play a ball horizontally off the face of a wall, it would travel to its left, the same amount as the ball would rise if played with the same club off level ground, because the trajectory would be merely "lying on its side". Now between the vertical wall and the horizontal level ground there is a right angle, therefore the wall represents a "ninety degrees slope". Bearing in mind that extreme example we can now consider the effects of a slope from which a golf ball *can* be played. From a twenty-two and a half degree slope (which is a quarter of the total ninety degrees) the ball will travel to the left the same fraction (one quarter) of the loft of the club used.

To clarify this I will tabulate some examples.

Slope.	Fraction of 90 degrees.	Club and loft, and elevation from level ground.	Ball's flight to the left.
90°	1	No. 3 Iron: 25°	Whole of 25° = 25°
45°	$\frac{1}{2}$	No. 3 Iron: 25°	Half of 25° = 12$\frac{1}{2}$°
45°	$\frac{1}{2}$	No. 5 Iron: 35°	Half of 35° = 17$\frac{1}{2}$°
45°	$\frac{1}{2}$	No. 7 Iron: 45°	Half of 45° = 22$\frac{1}{2}$°
30°	$\frac{1}{3}$	No. 3 Iron: 25°	Third of 25° = 8$\frac{1}{3}$°
30°	$\frac{1}{3}$	No. 5 Iron: 35°	Third of 35° = 11$\frac{2}{3}$°
30°	$\frac{1}{3}$	No. 7 Iron: 45°	Third of 45° = 15°
22$\frac{1}{2}$°	$\frac{1}{4}$	No. 3 Iron: 25°	Quarter of 25° = 6$\frac{1}{4}$°
22$\frac{1}{2}$°	$\frac{1}{4}$	No. 5 Iron: 35°	Quarter of 35° = 8$\frac{3}{4}$°
22$\frac{1}{2}$°	$\frac{1}{4}$	No. 7 Iron: 45°	Quarter of 45° = 11$\frac{1}{4}$°

Stated mathematically: as ninety degrees is to the slope, so is the loft of the club used, to the ball's flight leftwards, viz.:—

$$90° : \text{Slope} :: \text{Loft} : \text{Flight}.$$
$$\text{ex. } 90° : \ 30 \ :: \ 35 : \ X$$
$$\text{Therefore, } X = 11\frac{2}{3}°.$$

I hope the reader is not getting the impression that I am suggesting making these accurate calculations during play. I am merely trying to prove what happens with such a shot, so that he will know what to expect and how to get the best result.

Once the reader has grasped the principle involved, the whole matter becomes very simple. As he selects his club he thinks to himself:—"Ball higher than feet will go left, slope is quarter (say) of right angle, therefore aim right a quarter of club's loft." What could be easier? If even that calculation seems too complicated during play, it should be remembered that the consequent accuracy with a shot from such a lie to the green, might make all the difference to the result. Without it the ball could easily finish in a bunker to the left of the green, but with it, the ball might stop near the hole.

"The higher the ball is above the feet and the more the loft of the club, the more you must aim to the right"—is the nearest you can get to a working rule.

With the opposite lie, when the ball is below the feet, the same principle applies but in the opposite way, hence the acknowledged tendency for the ball to travel to the right—always erroneously called a slice instead of what it is, a "leaning trajectory". In this instance the player must aim the estimated distance to the left. It is probable that the ball will not go so far to the right from this lie, as it does to the left from the other. The reason is because it is an anatomical impossibility either to play a ball from so far "below" you, as it is high in front of you; or to swing the club head round to the right after impact, as it is round to the left of your body. That is to say, the trajectory cannot be made to lean so far to the right as it can to the left. The degree of the trajectory to the right, is governed by the degree the toe of the club head points "downwards" at address and impact. It is this last factor that the player will have to consider, when estimating the necessary correction in accordance with the rules formulated.

It should also be remembered that with a "leaning trajectory", whether to the right or left, the more it leans the less high will the ball go. In the hypothetical extreme example of playing a ball off the face of a wall (ninety degree slope), no matter which club is used the ball will not rise upwards at all.

This fact may seem unimportant, but it adds to our

store of knowledge, and also it could be important—and
would need to be taken into account—in playing over a
high obstacle such as a tree, from one of these lies.

A ball played from:	Rises to:
$\frac{3}{4}$ of 90° slope = 67$\frac{1}{2}$°	$\frac{1}{4}$ of normal height
$\frac{1}{2}$ of 90° slope = 45°	$\frac{1}{2}$ of normal height
$\frac{1}{4}$ of 90° slope = 22$\frac{1}{2}$°	$\frac{3}{4}$ of normal height

Stance and Address. Having decided where to aim, and
assumed a firm grip, take up a square stance in line with the
intended aim. Apply the club face to the ball so that the
club head rests—from toe to heel—on the ground. There
must be no cocking-up of the toe or heel of the club head—
except in those cases where the ball is so much lower than
the feet that it is anatomically impossible to ground the
club. With that one unusual exception, having got the
club head into the above correctly grounded position, you
will have had to bend your back more if the ball were low;
or unbend your back if the ball were high. Also you will
have had to stand nearer to the ball if it were low; and
farther from it if it were high. Lastly, you will have been
almost compelled to use a "long shaft" if the ball were low
and a short one if it were high. So much for the usual
"rules"—they happen!

Having got yourself into the really inevitable correct
position, you are now ready to commence the swing; but
first let us note a point or two regarding balance.

In the above described positions, with the ball below
your feet you should feel your weight distinctly on your
heels, with your seat protruding behind—almost in a sitting position. If you have not that feeling, then you are
too far from the ball. Don't correct this by stretching
your arms forward, but by moving your feet nearer the
ball.

With the ball above your feet, your weight should be more on your toes. If you have not that feeling, then you are too near the ball. Again, correct that by moving your feet. This position is one where "gripping the ground" with the toes might be indicated.

I will now demonstrate an anatomical fact which has a bearing on these shots. If a person stands erect, the angle formed at the "ankle" with the foot and the leg is approximately a right angle. If he puts more weight on to his heels, then that angle becomes more than a right angle; and with more weight on his toes it becomes less than a right angle. With the ankles in either of these positions, a wide stance will usually ensure better balance than will a narrow one.

The Swing. It is obvious that with the ball above the feet the swing will be flatter; and with the ball below the feet, it will be very upright.

Nevertheless, it is wise not to think of the swings as being different, but in both cases as merely a revolving of the shoulders around the upper part of the spine, by concentrating on the left shoulder as always. Reference to Diagram No. 13 will show that in both cases the player's chest and face "line" forms about a right angle with the line from the chest to the ball, as with normal shots.

I will forestall my critics among the better players, who may say about my description of "awkward lies"—"Too much unnecessary detail". They play these shots reasonably well, but it will not hurt them to understand how they do it—they might play even better! We all know how the high handicap player approaches these uneven lies. With no very definite idea of what to do, he curses his luck, carelessly "has a bash", which is usually anything but successful, then says to his partner, "What could you expect from *such* a lie?" He will now approach these shots in a different frame of mind, with the knowledge that he at least

knows what to do, and he will soon experience more
satisfaction than with the normal shot in having accomp-
plished something considered to be difficult.

(c) SHOTS FROM THE ROUGH

Playing from the "rough" is really a matter of common
sense. With the ball in any type of rough, the player
should ask himself the question: "In what direction must
the club head be travelling to most easily contact the ball?"
The answer will usually be obvious. All that is necessary
then, is to know the answer to that question.

The first thing to understand is that it is futile, in any
but the slighest rough, to attempt, in a normal manner, to
hit the ball in the back with a wide swing. I do not mean
that the swing is any different from that for an ordinary
shot—it is not—but the *ball position* is different, and consequently the ball is contacted earlier in the swing.

If we think of the rough as being various heights of
grass, shrubs, etc., growing upwards, then it is not difficult to understand that we should stand in such a position
in relationship to the ball, that the club head's journey to
the ball will be downwards (more or less), between the
grasses and shrubs, rather than against their sides, of
necessity near their stronger root-ends, where the ball will
be lying.

As already hinted the all-important factor is the stance,
and the consequent ball position in relationship to the feet.
I don't like open stances or open club faces, which are
supposed—by some authorities—to make the club head
offer less resistance to the grasses, but which actually only
add to the difficulty by complicating the ball position and
by reducing the available striking surface of the club, and
also the forward motion of it, thereby leaving much less
room for error, particularly when we could do with a
little more. Just as for the other shots, the square stance is

the most straightforward, the easiest to line up—and better in every way.

For practical purposes, and to facilitate description, we can divide "the Rough" into three degrees, each necessitating a different ball position. See Diagram No. 14, which represents the fairway, and the three degrees of rough, each with a ball near its roots. "R F" and "L F" are the right and left feet, put there for the purpose of demonstrating the ball positions. The four curves indicate—diagrammatically—the directions of the four forward swings up to impact. No. 1 is the normal ball position. No. 2—nearer the right than the left foot—is the ball position for the "first degree rough". No. 3—maybe slightly outside the right foot—is the ball position for the "second degree rough". No. 4—maybe six or even twelve inches outside the right foot—is the ball position for the "third degree rough".

The Four Rules. There are four important matters which if overlooked might spoil the shot, whatever the degree of rough.

1. Having assumed a firm grip, and put the feet into a comfortably wide square stance, stretch the left arm down and to the right when placing the club head just behind the ball. If the ball position should be outside the right foot, this will have the effect of pulling down the left shoulder to some extent, which is really appropriate to the club head being so far to the right. If you neglect to stretch the left arm, it is likely to collapse on the forward swing, causing the club face to shut too much, with a consequent pull to the left—or the ground may be struck behind the ball.

2. When applying the club head behind the ball, be sure to maintain the angle between your left arm and the club shaft, which will necessitate having the ball practically as far to your front as it would be for a normal shot. The

correctness of this will be recognised by the presence of a
slight bending—or "cocking"—at the left wrist, just as at
the normal address. Actually, as the club head is moved
farther and farther to the right, it does come gradually
nearer to you, but it must always be farther forward—i.e.,
to your "front"—than your hands. A common mistake
is to have the club shaft almost in line with the left arm,
pointing out to the right, and necessitating the ball being
too "near" to the player—i.e., not far enough to his front.
The probable result of this would be to strike the ball with
an open club face—pushing the ball out to the right.

3. When applying the club head behind the ball, see
that the face is square—i.e., at right angles to the anti-
cipated direction of flight and to your stance. To get the
club face into this correct position, it has to be more and
more shut, the farther the ball position is to the right.
This face shutting is tentatively done with the club normally in front of you before assuming the grip. Then, when
applied to the ball, if the face is not enough shut, it must be
further adjusted not by turning your hands and the club,
but by turning the club shaft in your hands while keeping
the hands in the same position.

4. It will be appreciated that as the ball position goes
farther to the right—necessitating the club face being
farther and farther shut, so the loft of the club face, and
consequently the ball elevation, becomes less and less.
For example, suppose you address the ball normally at
No. 1 position in the diagram with a niblick, then the club
would be approximately equivalent to a number six at No.
2 ball position; a number four iron at No. 3 ball position;
and a number two iron at No. 4 ball position. Knowing
this, it becomes apparent that in choosing the club for the
shot, you must be sure that there is some loft left on the
club—if possible—when behind the ball. For instance,
when playing from slight rough, you could probably use

any club appropriate to the distance required; but when it is necessary to have the ball farther to the right—say six or eight inches outside the right foot—you would probably need to use a niblick, and yet be left with the loft of only a number three iron.

However, you would still have twenty-five degrees of loft and elevation, and it is surprising with what little loft you can extract the ball if struck in the correct manner. But remember that if the ball is so far to the right that even the number nine has no available loft when the ball is addressed, then the chance of a successful shot will be negligible.

Briefly, then, the four points to be remembered when placing the club head behind the ball are: stretch the left arm; maintain the angle between the arm and club shaft; and use a club the face of which you can keep square to the target, and still have some available loft.

The Swing. Regarding the swing, there is, as usual, nothing to add to "left shoulder down, stop, left shoulder up", except that it is possible with some of the shots from the rough, when the ball is well outside the right foot, that some people will play the shot with more confidence simply by lifting the club up with the left arm and banging it down with the right one. Personally I prefer the "left shoulder swing" whenever possible, and would advise at least trying it first for even the most extreme degree of rough. By this means the player will learn at what ball position outside the right foot he must resort to the left-arm-up, right-arm-down movement.

"Rough Practice". The only way to learn to play from the rough with confidence is to practise these three shots with the three ball positions, without the rough. Play down the fairway from the uncut grass just off it. Don't practise them on the fairway, because you will invariably take a divot, and often a very large one; in fact, with some of the shots with the ball well outside the right foot the niblick will simply bury itself in the earth. Don't let this possibility put you off trying to swing right-through, which you will do more consistently if you commence the forward swing by pulling the left shoulder upwards.

When playing from the rough, more than ever is my advice necessary to grip very firmly.

You will soon know the pleasure, interest, and relative simplicity of these supposedly difficult shots. You should then look about the course for various degrees of rough into which to place your ball, and apply the principles which you have learnt to extract it. I know the result will surprise many, and particularly the distance they will often get—owing to the little remaining loft—from lies from which hitherto they had either scuffled the ball a few feet into a worse position, or missed it altogether.

Other Shots. It should be remembered that special types of shot may be required from the rough as from the fairway. For instance, if a shot should present an "uneven lie", then adjustments for this would be necessary just as on the fairway. Again, if a shot from the rough were very close to the green, it might be better played as a chip-shot with an open stance, as previously described; but nevertheless with the adjustments which the degree of rough demands.

The same principles can be applied to a shot—not from the rough, but owing to the fairway being soft or uneven —when the ball is in a bad or "cuppy" lie. The more deeply the ball is submerged, the farther to the right would it be positioned when addressing it. In addition, you will usually take a small divot before the ball, as well as a larger one afterwards.

There remains to be described one particular shot which is similar to, but different from, that from the third degree rough, when the ball position must be well outside the right foot. That is, when the ball lies maybe within a foot of a tree, hedge, or fence; thus preventing any form of normal back-swing.

Remember that with the most nearly vertical back-swing as described for a shot from the third degree rough, the club head is almost certain to go at least three feet farther to the right when waist high than when it was behind the ball at address, even with a "short grip". Therefore we must discover some way of causing the club head to rise on the back-swing practically vertically, or at any rate to travel less than a foot to the right of the ball.

Two possibilities should first be explored: the practicability of playing a cut-shot, or of playing a normal shot to the right of the desired line of flight when the desired line is at right angles to the fence or tree. If neither is feasible, then we must fall back on the following freak shot.

The widest back-swing is produced by making the upper part of the spine the hub; less wide by making the left shoulder-joint the hub; less again by using elbows and forearms, and still less by beginning the back-swing with hands and wrists. Obviously, we must apply this knowledge to the shot now under consideration.

First we must realise that the only club to use is that with the most loft—the number nine—because since it is going to rise and fall nearly vertically, therefore the ball position must be far outside the right foot. Consequently, there will be very little available loft left on the club—maybe only that of a number one iron—i.e., twenty degrees, or even less. It is necessary to have some loft and elevation, if only a few degrees.

Which of the three joints we use as the hub will depend on the space behind the ball to accommodate the "back-swing". To use the shoulder-joint you would normally need about three feet between the ball and the tree; for the elbow, one foot; and for the wrist only, six inches or even less. If those three measurements are remembered, then some sort of shot can always be attempted; but I prefer—shortly to be described—the method using always the same hub—the left shoulder—but with other modifications. I think it is obvious that the nearer the hub of the swing can be placed to the ground, the more nearly vertically can the club head be made to rise, but the loft will be further reduced.

We now have sufficient data to assume a suitable stance for this shot. Arrange your body and the club as you did for a third degree rough shot—i.e., square stance, with shut club face square to the line of flight just behind the ball, left arm stretched, which pulls the left shoulder down and to the right, with a slight bend at the wrist to place the club head reasonably to your front. In addition, so as to lower the hub nearer the ground, let the feet be three feet apart, and the left knee bent so that more weight is on the left foot. The back should be very bent, so that the hands are little more than a foot from the ground.

You are now ready to deliver the blow, by swinging either from the shoulder-joint, the elbow, or the wrist, depending on the distance available behind the ball. My own preference is to use the left shoulder-joint as the hub of the swing, if at all possible; that is, if it can be placed low enough to allow the "back-swing" to occur without striking the tree with the club head. Therefore, before striking the ball, perform a "quiet back-swing" to see if the club misses the tree or fence. If it does not, then bend the left knee more—so as to carry the left shoulder nearer the ground—until it does so. If it is not possible to get the left shoulder low enough to clear the tree, then you will have to be content with an "elbow or wrist swing", with either of which, it should be noted, it is more difficult to keep the back-swing on the correct line, and also there will be less power in the blow.

On the back-swing, it is very important to raise the club head on the line directly behind the ball, by which means you will obtain a more accurate blow than if the club head is allowed to go either inside or outside the line.

To execute the "swing", every part of your body except the arms should be kept perfectly still until the ball has gone. That is how it should feel, but in fact the body is bound to "give" a little. On the back-swing simply swing —or raise—your entire left arm from the shoulder-joint. If a longish back-swing is required there will probably be a little automatic wrist-cocking towards the end; also the left elbow will probably bend a little.

On the "forward"-swing—still keeping the rest of the body immovable—simply bang the club straight down with the right arm.

With this shot the ball usually rises from one to three feet into the air at the highest point in its trajectory; the maximum distance it travels being about seventy yards (yes, seventy!), while the average is forty to fifty yards. Shorter distances should be obtained by means of a shorter back-swing rather than a less forceful blow.

The same freak shot can be used from third degree rough, if the rough is such that you need a practically vertical "up and down" swing. Similarly, an "unplayable" ball can often be retrieved from the undergrowth under a tree or between trees on the edge of a wood.

Incidentally, this freak shot is the only shot in golf in which the forward-swing can truly be described as a down-swing.

(D) THE WEATHER

Dress suitably, to keep warm when it is cold, cool when it is hot, and dry when it is wet—if possible. I might complete this picture by saying "Keep wet when it is dry", but most golfers will not require advice on this matter of the nineteenth hole!

Sunshine. Golfers often complain about playing "into the sun", especially playing westwards in the late afternoon. Actually this should make them play better golf if they would do the sensible thing—viz., don't look up to see where the ball is going or has gone. Ask your opponent to watch the ball, then you can "stay down"—as you always should—until your left shoulder, your arms, and the club, going upwards, turn your head to the left. You will then usually find your ball in the middle of the fairway, or in such other position as you intended.

Wind. Wind does much more to the golfer than it does to the golf ball. The time-honoured advice to play low into the wind, and high with the wind; and to slice into a wind from the right, and hook into a wind from the left, does appear to be mathematically sound. But, since professionals appear to differ so much as to the necessity—and even desirability—for these adjustments, if you would simplify the rules I would suggest the following procedure.

If the wind is blowing against your back, aim slightly to the left (say to the left edge of the fairway); if it is blowing into your face, aim slightly to the right (say to the right edge of the fairway); otherwise ignore its effect on the ball.

The effect of wind on *you* is much more important, as it is very apt to upset your balance, than which there is nothing more vital in golf. Therefore, improve your grip of the ground by widening the stance. That alone, together with swinging upwards on the back-swing and upwards on the forward-swing—thus eliminating swaying—will take care of any wind blowing towards the sides of your body as you address the ball.

In addition to the wide stance, if the wind is blowing into

your face, grip the ground with your toes. That will have the effect of placing your weight slightly more on to your toes, so that the wind cannot blow you backwards; and the "ground gripping" will save you from any tendency to fall forwards. If the wind is blowing against your back, again lean into it, in this instance by putting your weight well on to your heels.

Rain and its Accompaniments. Apart from what has already been said, which might be applicable to the state of the terrain through rain, the only thing that matters, so far as golf is concerned, is to keep the club handles dry, or to dry them before use, as you cannot efficiently grip a wet club handle. There is one small—but important—matter: start every hole with a clean ball; and wipe the ball, if dirty, before putting. To get the best results with your "woods"—and to prolong their lives—wipe their heads dry after play.

Since "it is better to live to play another day", determine either to go on playing and get wet, or go home. Don't in any circumstances shelter under a lone tree. As Bill Kerr, the comedian, would say: "I don't want to 'wurry' you", but golfers are killed by lightning every year doing just that; and some of the older ones die from heart attacks or "strokes" when running for shelter. So get wet, and you will take no harm if you keep moving; and in any case, lightning is much more dangerous than pneumonia, especially since we now have penicillin and other modern "drugs".

The Golf Secret. If the reader wishes to acquire a professional grooved swing and to understand the many golf fallacies, he should read "THE GOLF SECRET" (uniform with this volume, from any bookseller; if difficulty, direct from the publishers).

INDEX

B. C. Macdonald's world famous individual models Repairs Series

FORD ESCORT REPAIRS
FORD CORTINA REPAIRS
BLMC MINI REPAIRS
BLMC 1100 AND 1300 REPAIRS
MORRIS MINOR 1000 REPAIRS

B. C. Macdonald, author of the best-seller "THE CAR DOCTOR", now applies all his knowledge and experience for the benefit of owners of the above named models. Each model range has its own book, but for reasons of space, high performance models in the ranges have had to be excluded.

He has evolved an entirely new formula in writing these books, which makes them easy for YOU to understand. The books are divided into ten Chapters, eight of which cover different parts of the car, each written on the same basic plan, i.e.,

Section 1: General data
Section 2: Fault symptoms
Section 3: Causes and cures. This section consists of the analytical step-by-step approach which has made B. C. Macdonald famous.
Section 4: and additional sections: special procedures for more complicated repairs and servicing, maintenance, etc.

Particular attention is paid to electrical faults, which without these books are most perplexing. An index allows instant reference to the place in the book where you will find what you want. Chapter 9 in each book deals with general maintenance and 10 gives additional data.

Each of the five books uniform with this volume

ELLIOT RIGHT WAY BOOKS
KINGSWOOD, SURREY, U.K.

LEARNING TO DRIVE IN PICTURES

by A. Tom Topper

The *first* book to really *attack* the difficulties simply and logically. The first quarter of this 208-page book – teaches absolute mastery of car control *to be* practised on open spaces or quiet, safe back streets. Step-by-step methods for achieving perfect three point turns, reverses into openings and hill starts (the three major bugbears) are all taught BEFORE throwing you in the deep end of thick traffic.

Many have been frightened off learning to drive by appalling instruction and trying to learn things far out of their depth to begin with. A few awful frights and the whole project seems to become a hysterical nightmare. All this can be avoided with Tom Topper, the master teacher.

THE AUTHOR DIAGNOSES DANGER MET IN DRIVING
THE ESSENTIAL MASTER-DRIVING LIFE-SAVING POINTS are not glossed over and ignored – each is emphasized and explained, so that a child of 12 could understand.

Wonderful reviews appeared on publication and here are some extracts:

The Times: 'Down-to-earth . . . practical . . . basic'
Daily Telegraph: 'For those who are still struggling . . . good value'
Daily Mirror: 'Clearer than many more expensive manuals'
The Sun: 'Admirable . . . amazingly cheap . . . invaluable'
Daily Sketch: 'Easiest to understand . . . excellent'
Woman's Own: 'Very helpful . . . gives all the theory'

More publicity was accorded when the 2nd edition appeared by the *Daily Mail*, *Woman's Own* again and London *Evening News*, etc.

The enormous 1st edition of six figures was sold within months under our famous 'Test pass or money back guarantee'. We had none returned.

Uniform with this volume